GETTING INSIDE
ANDROID

Beginner's Guide: Complete Android App
Development using Java Language

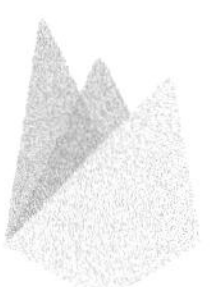

PREM KUMAR
ARCHANA PANDA

Disclaimer

This book is intended as a resource for individuals interested in Android app development. While every effort has been made to ensure the accuracy and completeness of the information provided, the author and publisher make no representations or warranties regarding the content's suitability, reliability, or correctness.

The material in this book is provided for informational purposes only. Android app development is a rapidly evolving field, and the techniques and technologies described within may become outdated over time. It is essential for readers to stay updated with the latest industry practices and guidelines.

The author and publisher shall not be held liable for any errors or omissions, or for any actions taken based on the information contained in this book. Readers are encouraged to exercise their own judgment and seek professional advice when necessary.

Furthermore, the author and publisher do not endorse any specific tools, libraries, or third-party products mentioned in this book. Mention of these items is for illustrative purposes and does not constitute an endorsement or recommendation.

The author and publisher reserve the right to update the content of this book in future editions to reflect changes in the field of Android app development.

Printed by Notion Press ©
Printed in India

Powered by F5 Developers ©
India

Author: Prem Kumar
Co-Author: Archana Panda

First Edition, 2023
ISBN

Dedication

This book is dedicated to the relentless spirit of innovation and the vibrant community of Android app developers around the world. Your passion for technology, your commitment to creating amazing user experiences, and your tireless pursuit of excellence inspire the pages within.

To the countless mentors, educators, and developers who generously share their knowledge, insights, and wisdom with others, this book stands as a tribute to your dedication to the craft and your willingness to uplift those who follow in your footsteps.

I also dedicate this book to my family and friends who provided unwavering support, encouragement, and understanding throughout the process of bringing these ideas to life. Your belief in me has been a constant source of motivation.

May this book serve as a valuable resource for aspiring and experienced Android app developers alike, and may it contribute, in some small way, to the continued growth and innovation of the Android ecosystem.

Thank you all for being a part of this journey.

CONTENTS

Foreword

"Our lives will be facilitated by a myriad of adaptive applications running on different devices, with different sensors, all of them collecting tidbits about everything we do, and feeding big digital brains that can adapt applications to our needs simply because they get to know us."

— Márcio Cyrillo

In the ever-evolving landscape of technology, mobile app development has emerged as a driving force, enabling us to connect, create, and innovate like never before. In this dynamic field, Android stands out as a powerful platform that has reshaped the way we interact with our devices and the digital world.

I am honored to write the foreword for this exceptional book on Android app development. As someone deeply immersed in the world of technology and software development, I have witnessed firsthand the remarkable growth of the Android ecosystem and the incredible potential it holds. In these pages, you will find a comprehensive and insightful guide to mastering the art and science of Android app development. The author's expertise and dedication shine through, making this book an invaluable resource for both beginners looking to embark on their app development journey and seasoned professionals seeking to refine their skills.

What sets this book apart is its commitment to clarity, depth, and practicality. The author has taken great care to explain complex concepts in a straightforward manner, providing readers with a clear roadmap to building Android apps that are not only functional but also user-friendly and engaging.

Whether you're exploring Android development for the first time or seeking to elevate your existing skills, you'll discover a wealth of knowledge, best practices, and real-world insights within these pages. From the fundamentals of Android architecture to advanced techniques for crafting compelling user interfaces and optimizing performance, this book covers it all.

I encourage you to dive into this book with enthusiasm and an open mind. Embrace the challenges and opportunities of Android app development, for it is a field that rewards creativity, persistence, and a commitment to continuous learning. By the time you reach the final chapter, you'll have gained the skills and confidence needed to embark on your own Android app development projects.

It is my sincere belief that this book will serve as an indispensable companion on your journey to becoming a proficient Android app developer. May it empower you to create apps that enrich the lives of users, drive innovation, and contribute to the ever-expanding world of Android.

Congratulations to the author for crafting this outstanding resource, and best wishes to all readers as you embark on your Android app development adventures.

Prem Kumar
India Book of Records Holder

Acknowledgments

Writing a book is a labor of love, and it takes a village to bring it to fruition. I want to express my heartfelt gratitude to all those who have been instrumental in making this Android app development book a reality.

First and foremost, I want to thank my family for their unwavering support and patience during the countless hours I spent researching, writing, and editing. Your encouragement has been my motivation.

I extend my deepest appreciation to my mentors and colleagues in the field of Android app development. Your guidance, insights, and willingness to share knowledge have enriched this book and my understanding of the subject.

I am grateful to the Android developer community, a vibrant and collaborative group that continually pushes the boundaries of what's possible on the platform. Your passion for innovation has inspired the content of this book.

I want to acknowledge the contributions of the co-author of this book, Mrs. Archana Panda who worked tirelessly to proofread the book to ensure we can deliver the best to the readers. Thank you for bringing in your experience to transform the manuscript into a polished book. Your professionalism and dedication are deeply appreciated.

To the countless open-source contributors and developers who create the tools, libraries, and frameworks that power Android app development, you are the backbone of this ecosystem. Your work has enabled developers like me to bring ideas to life.

Finally, a special thank you to the person, whose presence only keeps me motivated. Your unwavering support and understanding made it possible for me to focus on this project.

This book would not have been possible without the collective efforts and support of all these individuals and groups. Thank you for being part of this journey.

Introduction

Welcome to the exciting world of Android app development! In an era where smartphones have become an integral part of our lives, the ability to create powerful and user-friendly mobile applications is an invaluable skill. Whether you're a beginner looking to embark on your journey into Android app development or an experienced developer seeking to expand your expertise, this book is your comprehensive guide to mastering the art and science of building Android apps.

A World of Possibilities

Android, the world's most popular mobile operating system, offers a vast and dynamic platform for innovation. With Android, you have the opportunity to create apps that can transform ideas into reality, solve problems, and connect people across the globe.

Why This Book?

You might be wondering why you should choose this book as your guide on this exciting journey. The answer lies in its comprehensive and hands-on approach. We've designed this book to take you from the fundamentals of Android app development to advanced techniques used by industry professionals.

Whether you're interested in building your first app or fine-tuning your existing skills, you'll find valuable insights, practical examples, and real-world projects to guide you every step of the way.

What You'll Learn

Here's a glimpse of what you can expect to learn from this book:

- **Android Fundamentals:** We'll start with the basics, including an introduction to the Android platform, its history, and its core components.
- **Getting Started:** You'll set up your development environment, learn about the Android Studio IDE, and build your first "Hello World" app.
- **User Interface Design:** Discover the principles of effective UI/UX design and how to create visually appealing and user-friendly interfaces.
- **Data Storage and Retrieval:** Explore various techniques for storing and retrieving data, including SQLite databases, shared preferences, and cloud-based solutions.
- **Networking and APIs:** Learn how to connect your app to the internet, retrieve data from web services, and integrate APIs seamlessly.
- **Advanced Topics:** Dive into advanced topics such as background processing, location-based services, and material design.
- **Testing and Debugging:** Master the art of testing and debugging your apps to ensure they run smoothly.
- **Publishing Your App:** Finally, we'll guide you through the process of publishing your app on the Google Play Store, making it available to millions of users worldwide.

Who Is This Book For?

This book is designed to cater to a wide audience, including:

- Beginners with little or no prior programming experience looking to start a career in Android app development.
- Experienced developers from other platforms eager to transition to Android.
- Seasoned Android developers seeking to enhance their skills and stay up-to-date with the latest trends and best practices.

Let's Get Started

The journey to becoming a proficient Android app developer begins now. Each chapter of this book will provide you with valuable insights, practical examples, and hands-on exercises to build your skills and confidence. It's time to roll up your sleeves, fire up Android Studio, and embark on this exciting adventure.

Are you ready to create incredible Android apps that could change the world? Let's dive in!

PART 1

Getting Through the Development Kit

CHAPTER 1

GETTING INSIDE ANDROID

Why Android?

Android is the best-selling open-source Linux-based operating system among various mobile platforms across the globe. Hundreds of millions of mobile devices are powered by Android in more than 190 countries of the world. It conquered around 70.8% of the global market share by the end of August 2023, and this trend is growing bigger every other day.

The story of Android dates back to 2003 when Andy Rubin, Rich Miner, Nick Sears, and Chris White co-founded a start-up Android Inc. in Palo Alto, California. However, the company was later faced with the insufficiency of funds which brought Google into the picture. Google could sense the potential the product carried within and sealed a deal worth $50 Million to acquire Android in 2005. All the four Co-founders soon moved to the Googleplex to continue to develop the OS further under their new owners. The first public Android Beta Version 1.0 was finally published on 5th November 2007.

Android has the potential for removing the barriers to success in the development and sale of a new generation of mobile phone application software. Just as the standardized PC and Macintosh platforms created markets for desktop and server software, Android, by providing a standard mobile phone application environment, will create a market for mobile applications—and the opportunity for applications developers to profit from those applications.

The Open Handset Alliance

Google and 33 other companies announced the formation of the Open Handset Alliance on November 5, 2007 (currently, 84 companies are part of the alliance). According to the joint press release from that day:

This alliance shares a common goal of fostering innovation on mobile devices and giving consumers a far better user experience than much of what is available on today's mobile platforms. By providing developers a new level of openness that enables them to work more collaboratively, Android will accelerate the pace at which new and compelling mobile services are made available to consumers.

For us as mobile application developers, that means we are free to develop whatever creative mobile applications we can think of, free to market them (or give them, at our option) to Android mobile phone owners, and free to profit from that effort any way we can. Each member of the Open Handset Alliance has its own reasons for participating and contributing its intellectual property, and we are free to benefit.

The Open Handset Alliance integrates contributed software and other intellectual property from its member companies and makes it available to developers through the open source community. Software is licensed through the Apache V2 license, which you can see at http://www.apache.org/licenses/LICENSE-2.0.txt. Use of the Apache license is critical, because it allows handset manufacturers to take Android code, modify it as necessary, and then either keep it proprietary or release it back to the open source community, at their option. The original Alliance members include handset manufacturers (HTC, LG, Motorola, Samsung), mobile operators (China Mobile Communications, KDDI, DoCoMo, Sprint/Nextel, T-Mobile, Telecom Italia, Telefonica), semiconductor companies (Audience, Broadcom, Intel, Marvell, NVidia Qualcomm, SiRF, Synaptics), software companies (Ascender, eBay, esmertec, Google, LivingImage, LiveWire, Nuance, Packet Video, SkyPop, SONiVOX), and commercialization companies (Aplix, Noser, TAT, Wind River). The Alliance includes the major partners needed to deliver a platform for mobile phone applications in all of the major geographies. There are other firms as well which were on boarded as a part of the alliance in between (currently, 84 firms are part of the alliance).

The Alliance releases software through Google's developer website (http://developer.android.com). The Android SDK for use by application software developers can be downloaded directly from that website. (The Android Platform Porting Kit for use by handset manufacturers who want to port the Android platform to a handset design.)

Versions of Android

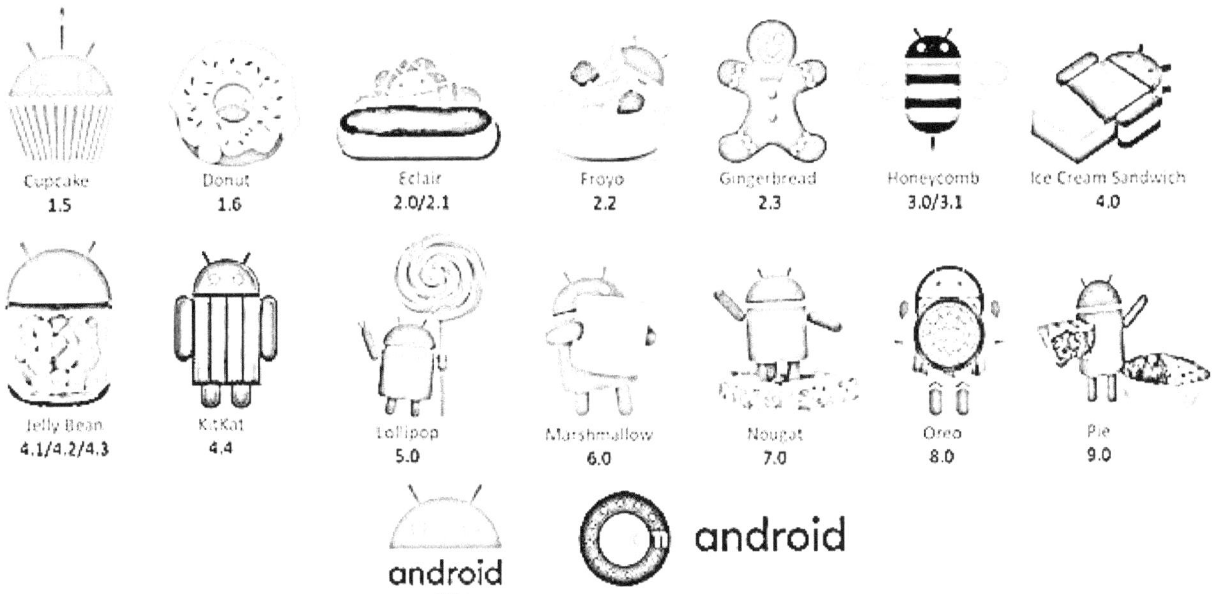

- **Android 1.0 to 1.1: No codename**

In September 2008, Android officially released Android version 1.0. It is the very first version of the Android operating system. It includes a web browser that can display HTML and XHTML web pages, a camera, and a connection to an online email server (POP3, IMAP4, and SMTP).

Google Calendar, Google Sync, Google Maps, Google Search, Google Talk, Instant messaging, Media player, Notifications display in the status bar, background, YouTube video player, Alarm Clock, Calculator, Dialer, Pictures (Gallery), Wi-Fi and Bluetooth support are all included in this version.

- **Android 1.5: Cupcake**

On April 27, 2009, Android 1.5 was released with the codename dessert item (Cupcake). It runs the Linux kernel 2.6.27. It includes a third-party virtual keyboard, MPEG-4 video recording, playback, a copy, and paste tool, animated screen translations, an auto-rotation option, the ability to post a movie to YouTube, photographs to Picasa, and the ability to view phone usage history.

- **Android 1.6: Donut**

Android 1.6, codenamed Donut, was released on September 15, 2009. It has various new features such as voice and text entry search, bookmark history, contacts, web, say a string of text, faster camera access, the ability to choose multiple photographs for deletion, text-to-speech engine support, and WVGA screen resolutions.

- **Android 2.0 to 2.1: Eclair**

Android 2.0, codenamed Eclair, was released on October 26, 2009. It was built with the Linux kernel 2.6.29. It includes several new features such as expansive account sync, Microsoft Exchange email support, Bluetooth 2.1, the ability to tap a Contact photo and select to call, SMS, the ability to search all saved SMS, MMS messages, the ability to delete the earliest message automatically when the described limit is reached, Minor API, and minor bug fixed.

- **Android 2.2 to 2.2.3: Froyo**

Android 2.2 (Froyo) was released on May 20, 2010, on the Linux kernel 2.6.32. It has several features such as speed, memory, and performance optimization. JIT compilation, JavaScript engine into the Browser application, integration of Chrome's V8, support for Android Cloud to Device Messaging service, security upgrades, Adobe Flash support, and speed improvements are all included.

- **Android 2.3 to 2.3.7: Gingerbread**

Android 2.3 (Gingerbread) was released on December 6, 2010, on the Linux kernel 2.6.35. It now supports extra-large screen sizes, has a revised user interface design with better simplicity and efficiency, enhanced copy/paste capability, chooses a word by press-holding, supports Near Field Communication (NFC), headphone virtualization, and a new Download Manager. It has improved Nexus S bug fixes, audio or video chat with Google Talk, network performance for Nexus S 4G, Gmail app, battery efficiency, addressed a voice search bug and added Google Wallet compatibility for Nexus S 4G.

- **Android 3.0 to 3.2.6: Honeycomb**

Android 3.0 (Honeycomb) was released on February 22, 2011, for the first Android tablet based on the Linux kernel 2.6.36.

It includes features such as a holographic user interface for tablets, added system Bar, simplified multitasking by tapping Recent Application in the System Bar, a redesign of the keyboard for faster typing, hardware acceleration, quick access to camera exposure, support for multi-core processors, UI refinements, connectivity for USB accessories, support for joysticks and gamepads, a high-performance Wi-Fi lock, improved hardware support, Google Books, and a fix for data connectivity issues with Bluetooth.

- **Android 4.0 to 4.0.4: Ice Cream Sandwich**

Android 4.0.1 (Ice Cream Sandwich) was released on October 19, 2011, and was based on the Linux kernel 3.0.1. It was the last version of the Adobe System Flash player that was officially supported.

It introduces a slew of new features, including refinements to the Holo interface, a new Roboto font family, the separation of widgets in a new tab, integrated screenshot capture, improved error correction on the keyboard, improved copy and pastes functionality, a built-in photo editor, minor bug fixes, graphics improvements, spell-checking, and improved camera performance.

- **Android 4.1 to 4.3.1: Jelly Bean**

Google launched Android 4.1 (Jelly Bean) during the Google I/O conference on June 27, 2012. It is built on the Linux kernel 3.0.31.

It includes the following updates: a smoother user interface, improved accessibility, expandable notifications, a bug fix for the Nexus 7, one-finger gestures to expand/collapse notifications, lock screen improvements, multiple user accounts (tablets only), a new clock app, Bluetooth low energy support, volume for incoming calls, 4K resolution support, native emoji support, and bug fixes for the Nexus 7 LTE.

- **Android 4.4 to 4.4.4: KitKat**

Google released Android 4.4 on September 3, 2013. (KitKat). Its code name was initially "Key Lime Pie." On October 31, 2013, Google began on Google's Nexus 5. The amount of RAM that Android should have is at least 340 MB.

Other devices which have less than 512 MB of RAM must be reported as low RAM devices. It includes new features such as a clock that no longer displays bold hours, wireless printing capability, WebViews based on the Chromium engine, sensor batching, a built-in screen recording feature, improved application compatibility, and a camera application that loads Google+ Photo rather than Gallery.

- **Android 5.0 to 5.1.1: Lollipop**

On June 25, 2014, Android L was renamed Lollipop. On November 12, 2014, it was formally unveiled. Lollipop includes a redesigned user interface, support for 64-bit CPUs, print previews, material design, Project Volta for improved device battery life, multiple user accounts, audio input and output via USB devices, join Wi-Fi networks, support for multiple SIM cards, high-definition voice calls, device protection, and native Wi-Fi calling support.

- **Android 6.0 - 6.0.1: Marshmallow**

On May 28, 2015, the Android 6.0 Marshmallow was released under the codename Android M for the Nexus 5 and 6 phones and the Nexus 9 tablet.

Android Marshmallow was released on October 5, 2015, for all Android smartphones. It includes new features like App Standby, Dozes mode to save battery life, native fingerprint reader support, runtime permission requests, USB-C connectivity, and Unicode 7.0 & 8.0 emoji support.

- **Android 7.0 to 7.1.2: Nougat**

The Android operating system's major release was Nougat. The initial codename for it was Android N. On March 9, 2016, it was released as a developer preview and factory images for the Nexus device.

The final preview build was released on August 22, 2016, with the following features: file-based encryption, screen zoom, multi-window support, new Data Saver mode, JIT compiler makes app installation 75 percent faster, picture-in-picture support, support manager APIs, circular app icon support, send GIFs directly from the default keyboard, battery usage alerts.

- **Android 8.0 to 8.1: Oreo**

Android 8.0 Oreo was the Android operating system's eighth major version. On March 21, 2017, it was initially made available for developer preview. On July 24, 2017, the final developer preview was made public.

On August 21, 2017, its stable version was released, which included several features such as picture-in-picture support, support for Unicode 10.0 emoji (5.0), restructured settings, adaptive icons, notification channels, notification dots, two times faster boot time, Google Play Protect, Integrated printing support, Neural network API, shared memory API, Android Oreo Go Edition, autofill framework, automatic light, and dark themes, and more.

- **Android 9.0: Pie**

Android 9.0 Pie was the Android operating system's ninth major version. Google first announced it and released a preview version on March 7, 2018. On August 6, 2018, it was officially released. The clock has been shifted to the left of the notification bar, a screenshot button has been added, and the battery % is always displayed.

- **Android 10**

Android 10 is the tenth version of the Android operating system. Android 10 is being developed under the codename Android Q. Google first announced it on March 13, 2019, and its first beta version was released on the same day, followed by its second beta on April 3, 2019.

On September 3, 2019, Android 10's stable version was launched. It has new rights to access location in the background, a floating settings panel, support for an AV1 video codec, fingerprint authentication support, and WPA3 Wi-Fi security.

- **Android 11**

Android 11 is the eleventh big release of the Android operating system. It is the 18th version of the Android mobile operating system, released on September 8, 2020. Since Android 10, the alphabetic naming system based on deserts has been discontinued. As a result, this operating system has been labeled Android 11.

It includes features like Conversation, Accessibility where you can navigate through voice commands. Device controls for maintaining all devices in one place and privacy give more security to using a smartphone in today's generation.

- **Android 12**

Android 12 is the twelfth big release and the nineteenth version of Android, the mobile operating system created by the Open Handset Alliance, led by Google. On May 18, 2021, the first beta was released. Android 12 was made available to the public on October 4, 2021, via the Android Open Source Project (AOSP) and was made available to supported Google Pixel devices on October 19, 2021.

It includes features like User Interface, including larger buttons, more animation, and a new look for home screen widgets. System services such as the WindowManager, system server, PackageManager, and interrupts have all seen performance boosts.

- **Android 13**

Tiramisu, the codename for Android 13, is a planned major update of the Android smartphone operating system. On February 10, 2022, the first preview version was released.

First, the split-screen has a somewhat different UI, with rounded corners on the two apps. Although no apps use it, a new photo picker is launched. The Quick Settings pulldown animation has been modified, tiny modifications have been made to popup windows and the media player, and vibration can now be turned off completely. The user's function has been enhanced, with the ability to choose which specific user can access apps. To safeguard privacy, none of the apps will include any sensitive information. This version allows third-party apps to use themed (monochrome) icons.

Android Fundamentals

To start with android development, you need to go through some prerequisites which will be beneficial in development phase. You have to go through the OOPs concept, need to learn the 4 main components of android (will discuss in detail in upcoming chapters) and basic knowledge about programming. Let us go through some fundamentals of Android:

- **Android Programming Languages**

In Android, basically, programming is done in two languages JAVA or C++ and XML(Extension Markup Language). Nowadays KOTLIN is also preferred (in this book, Java will be used for programming). The XML file deals with the design, presentation, layouts, blueprint, etc (as a front-end) while the JAVA or KOTLIN deals with the working of buttons, variables, storing, etc (as a back-end).

- **Android Components**

The App components are the building blocks of Android. Each component has its own role and life cycles i.e from launching of an app till the end. Some of these components depend upon others also. Each component has a definite purpose. The four major app components are:

    i.   Activities
    ii. Services
    iii. Broadcast Receivers
    iv. Content Provider

Activities: It deals with the UI and the user interactions to the screen. In other words, it is a User Interface that contains activities. These can be one or more depending upon the App. It starts when the application is launched. At least one activity is always present which is known as MainActivity. The activity is implemented through the following.

Syntax:

```
public class MainActivity extends Activity{

  // processes

}
```

Services: Services are the background actions performed by the app, these might be long-running operations like a user playing music while surfing the Internet. A service might need other sub-services so as to perform specific tasks. The main purpose of the Services is to provide non-stop working of the app without breaking any interaction with the user.

Syntax:

```
public class MyServices extends Services{

  // code for the services

}
```

Broadcast Receivers: A Broadcast is used to respond to messages from other applications or from the System. For example, when the battery of the phone is low, then the Android OS fires a Broadcasting message to launch the Battery Saver function or app, after receiving the message the appropriate action is taken by the app. Broadcast Receiver is the subclass of BroadcastReceiver class and each object is represented by Intent objects.

Syntax:

```
public class MyReceiver extends BroadcastReceiver{

   public void onReceive(context,intent){

 }
```

Content Provider: Content Provider is used to transferring the data from one application to the others at the request of the other application. These are handled by the class ContentResolver class. This class implements a set of APIs(Application Programming Interface) that enables the other applications to perform the transactions. Any Content Provider must implement the Parent Class of ContentProvider class.

Syntax:

```
public class MyContentProvider extends ContentProvider{

   public void onCreate()

   {}

}
```

- **Structural Layout Of Android Studio**

The basic structural layout of Android Studio is given below:

Manifest Folder: Android Manifest is an XML file that is the root of the project source set. It describes the essential information about the app and the Android build tools, the Android Operating System, and Google Play. It contains the permission that an app might need in order to perform a specific task. It also contains the Hardware and the Software features of the app, which determines the compatibility of an app on the Play Store. It also includes special activities like services, broadcast receiver, content providers, package name, etc.

Java Folder: The JAVA folder consists of the java files that are required to perform the background task of the app. It consists of the functionality of the buttons, calculation, storing, variables, toast (small popup message), programming function, etc. The number of these files depends upon the type of activities created.

Resource Folder: The res or Resource folder consists of the various resources that are used in the app. This consists of sub-folders like drawable, layout, mipmap, raw, and values. The drawable consists of the images. The layout consists of the XML files that define the user interface layout. These are stored in res.layout and are accessed as R.layout class. The raw consists of the Resources files like audio files or music files, etc. These are accessed through R.raw.filename. values are used to store the hardcoded strings(considered safe to store string values) values, integers, and colors. It consists of various other directories like:

R.array :*arrays.xml* for resource arrays
R.integer : *integers.xml* for resource integers
R.bool : *bools.xml* for resource boolean
R.color :*colors.xml* for color values
R.string : *strings.xml* for string values
R.dimen : *dimens.xml* for dimension values
R.style : *styles.xml* for styles

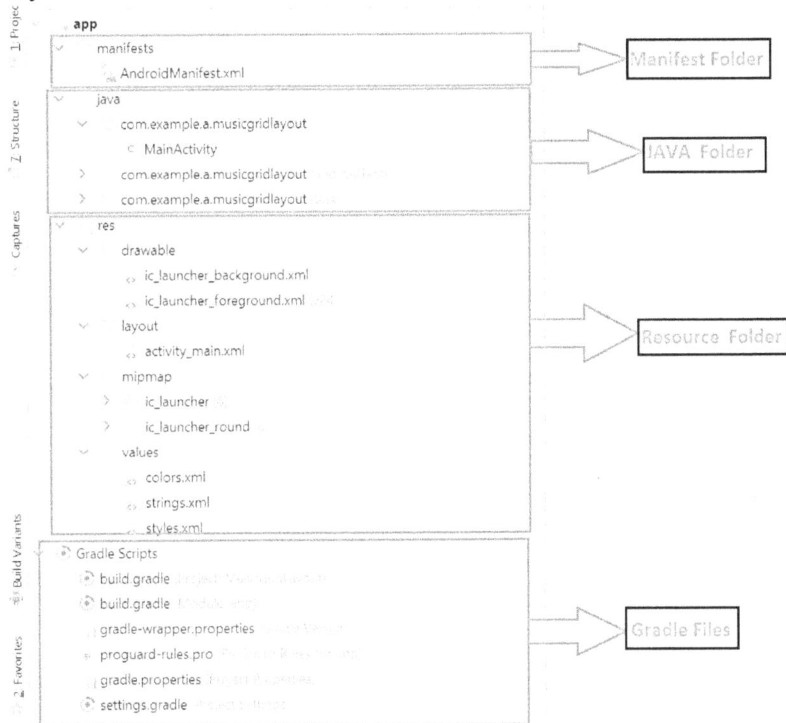

Gradle Files: Gradle is an advanced toolkit, which is used to manage the build process, that allows defining the flexible custom build configurations. Each build configuration can define its own set of code and resources while reusing the parts common to all versions of your app.

The Android plugin for Gradle works with the build toolkit to provide processes and configurable settings that are specific to building and testing Android applications. Gradle and the Android plugin run independently of Android Studio. This means that you can build your Android apps from within Android Studio. The flexibility of the Android build system enables you to perform custom build configurations without modifying your app's core source files.

Android Activity Lifecycle

Android is designed around the unique requirements of mobile applications. In particular, Android recognizes that resources (memory and battery, for example) are limited on most mobile devices, and provides mechanisms to conserve those resources.

The mechanisms are evident in the Android Activity Lifecycle, which defines the states or events that an activity goes through from the time it is created until it finishes running.

States of Android Lifecycle:

- OnCreate: This is called when activity is first created.
- OnStart: This is called when the activity becomes visible to the user.
- OnResume: This is called when the activity starts to interact with the user.
- OnPause: This is called when activity is not visible to the user.
- OnStop: This is called when activity is no longer visible.
- OnRestart: This is called when activity is stopped, and restarted again.
- OnDestroy: This is called when activity is to be closed or destroyed.

Detailed introduction on each method with programming examples will be discussed in the part 2 of the book.

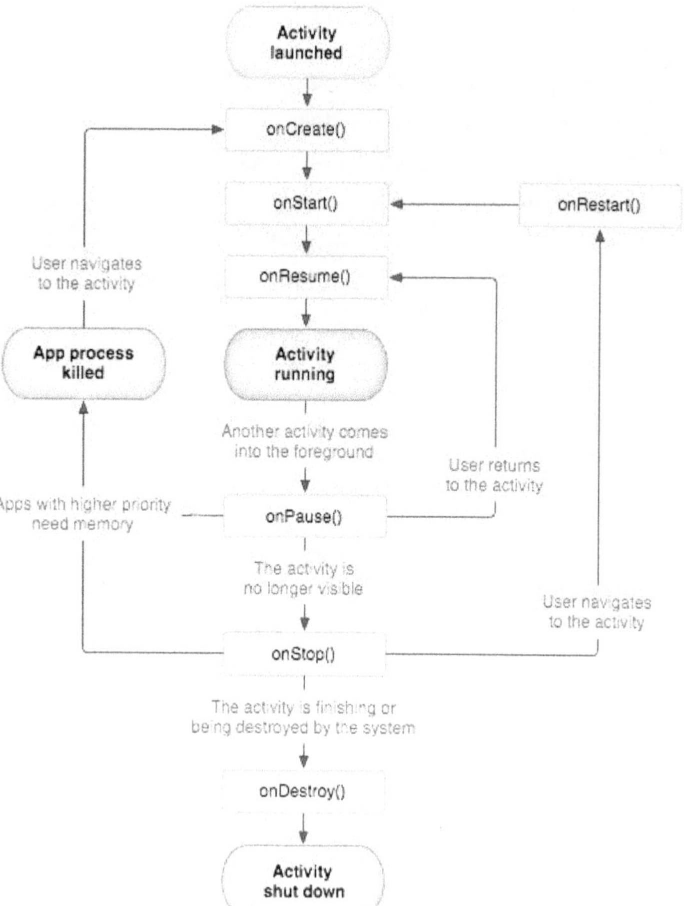

Android Architecture

An Android operating system for touchscreen devices poses a number of challenges that must be overcome when developing it. So, in a way, the architecture for an Android platform consists of a set of software components designed to support a large number of Android-enabled devices. This mobile operating system is based on a layered architecture of software stacks comprising a Linux kernel, a runtime environment, supporting libraries, an application framework, as well as a set of applications. As part of building such a complex system, careful structural attention must be paid to make sure all the Android Architect components do not conflict with each other. The Android architecture protects its many components from crashing altogether while keeping their independent functionalities intact. Some of the benefits of Android's layered architecture can be summed up as follows:

- With a layered Android architecture, it will ensure that different problems will be broken down and will be dealt with on different levels.
- Android software developers can avoid low-level problems each time they develop by using a layered architecture. Instead, they can focus on delivering business value relating to the layer they are working on, rather than working on the details.
- There is no need for developers who are working on developing apps to be concerned about the actual implementation of the application framework. Such responsibilities will fall to system developers responsible for implementing the application framework.
- Since Android has a layered structure, it is possible to apply updates incorporating bug fixes or improvements to each layer independently. Keeping changes within layers independent is crucial to ensuring that their effects are not intertwined with one another.
- Developers at different levels of an operating system are able to work together without getting in each other's way. This is particularly important when updating and publishing new versions of an operating system.

The main components of android architecture are following:-

i. Applications
ii. Application Framework
iii. Android Runtime
iv. Platform Libraries
v. Linux Kernel

Below is the graphical representation of android architecture with several main components and their sub components:

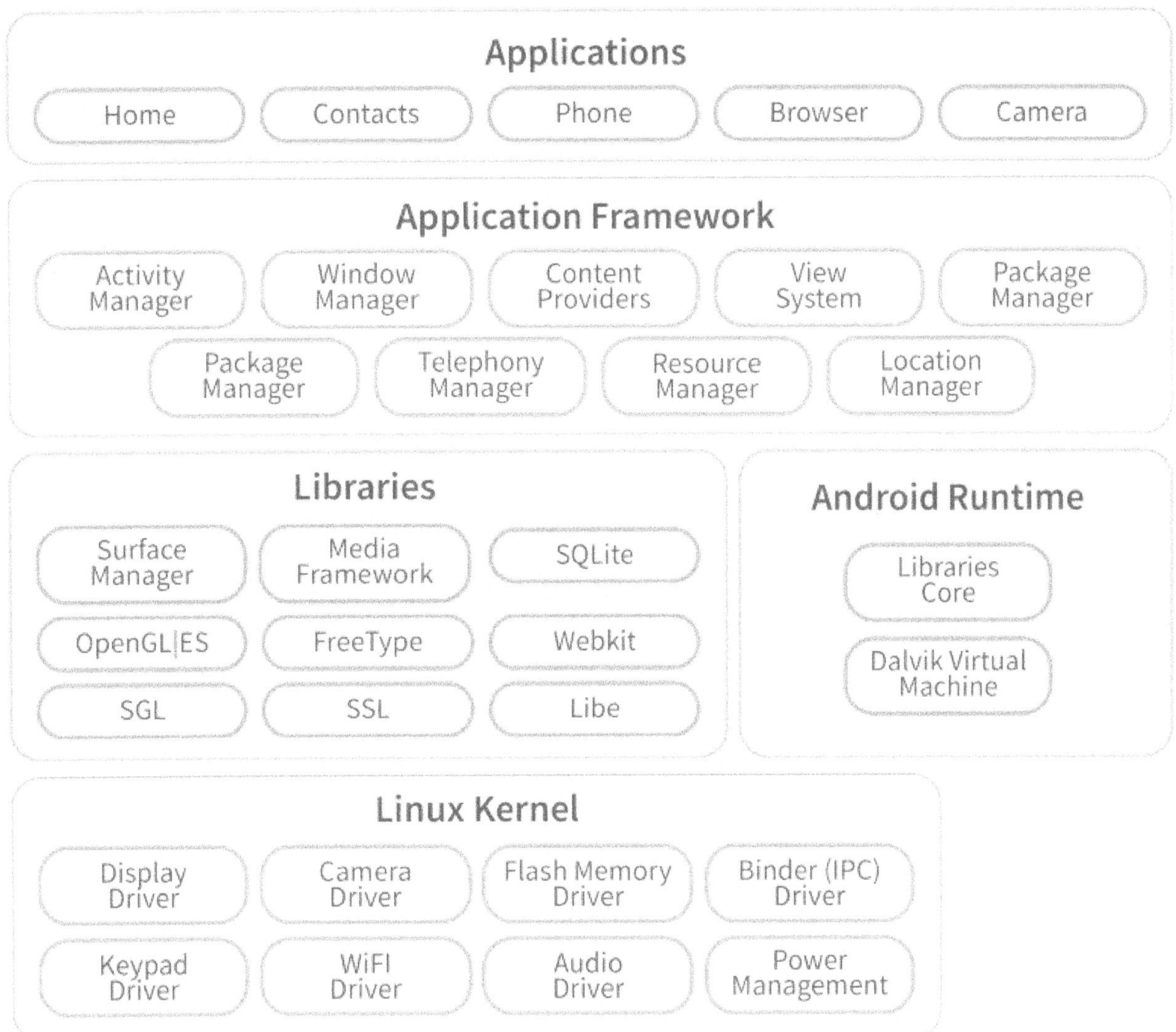

Applications:

- Applications is the top layer of android architecture. The pre-installed applications like home, contacts, camera, gallery etc and third party applications downloaded from the play store like chat applications, games etc. will be installed on this layer only.
- It runs within the Android run time with the help of the classes and services provided by the application framework.

Application framework:

- Application Framework provides several important classes which are used to create an Android application.
- It provides a generic abstraction for hardware access and also helps in managing the user interface with application resources.
- Generally, it provides the services with the help of which we can create a particular class and make that class helpful for the Applications creation.
- It includes different types of services activity manager, notification manager, view system, package manager etc. which are helpful for the development of our application according to the prerequisite.

Application runtime:

- Android Runtime environment is one of the most important part of Android.
- It contains components like core libraries and the Dalvik virtual machine (DVM).
- Mainly, it provides the base for the application framework and powers our application with the help of the core libraries.
- Like Java Virtual Machine (JVM), Dalvik Virtual Machine (DVM) is a register-based virtual machine and specially designed and optimized for android to ensure that a device can run multiple instances efficiently. It depends on the layer Linux kernel for threading and low-level memory management.
- The core libraries enable us to implement android applications using the standard JAVA or Kotlin programming languages.

Platform libraries:

- The Platform Libraries includes various C/C++ core libraries and Java based libraries such as Media, Graphics, Surface Manager, OpenGL etc. to provide a support for android development.

    o **Media** library provides support to play and record an audio and video formats.
    o **Surface manager** responsible for managing access to the display subsystem.
    o **SGL** and **OpenGL** both cross-language, cross-platform application program interface (API) are used for 2D and 3D computer graphics.
    o **SQLite** provides database support and **FreeType** provides font support.
    o **Web-Kit** This open source web browser engine provides all the functionality to display web content and to simplify page loading.
    o **SSL (Secure Sockets Layer)** is security technology to establish an encrypted link between a web server and a web browser.

Linux Kernel:

- Linux Kernel is heart of the android architecture. It manages all the available drivers such as display drivers, camera drivers, Bluetooth drivers, audio drivers, memory drivers, etc. which are required during the runtime.
- The Linux Kernel will provide an abstraction layer between the device hardware and the other components of android architecture.
- It is responsible for management of memory, power, devices etc.

The features of Linux kernel are:

- **Security:** The Linux kernel handles the security between the application and the system.
- **Memory Management:** It efficiently handles the memory management thereby providing the freedom to develop our apps.

- **Process Management:** It manages the process well, allocates resources to processes whenever they need them.
- **Network Stack:** It effectively handles the network communication.
- **Driver Model:** It ensures that the application works properly on the device and hardware manufacturers responsible for building their drivers into the Linux build.

CHAPTER 2

SETTING UP ANDROID DEVELOPMENT ENVIRONMENT

Android applications, like most mobile phone applications, are developed in a host target development environment. In other words, you develop your application on a host computer (where resources are abundant) and download it to a target mobile phone for testing and ultimate use. Applications can be tested and debugged either on a real Android device or on an emulator. For most developers, using an emulator is easier for initial development and debugging, followed by final testing on real devices.

To write your own Android mobile phone applications, you'll first need to collect the required tools and set up an appropriate development environment on your PC or Mac. In this chapter we'll collect the tools you need, download them and install them on your computer, and write a sample application that will let you get the feel of writing and running Android applications on an emulator. Linux, Windows, and OS X are all supported development environments, and we'll show you how to install the latest set of tools on each. Then, we'll show you any configuration you need to do after installing the tools (setting PATH environment variables and the like), again for each of the three operating systems. Finally, we'll write a short little "Hello, Android" application that demonstrates what needs to be done in order to get a generic application running.

The Android SDK supports several different integrated development environments (IDEs). For this book we will focus on Android Studio because it is the IDE that is best integrated with the SDK and optimized for android apps, and, hey, it's free. No matter which operating system you are using, you will need essentially the same set of tools:

• The Android Studio IDE

• Sun's Java Development Kit (JDK)

Creating an Android Development Environment

Setting up a Suitable Development Environment is necessary before one can begin creating Android Applications. It makes it easier for developers to use the tools required to create any Application and ensures that all Operations or Processes run smoothly.

The Android Software Development Kit supports Windows, Linux and Mac OS X (10.4.8 or later, Intel platform only) as host development environments. Installation of the SDK is substantially the same for any of the operating systems, and most of this description applies equally to all of them. Where the procedure differs, we will clearly tell you what to do for each environment:

Installing JDK

The Android SDK requires latest version of JDK. If you already have one of those installed, skip to the next step. In particular, JDK can be installed on different platforms i.e., Windows, Linux or Mac OS. If the JDK is not installed, go to https://www.oracle.com/java/technologies/downloads/ and you'll see a list of Java products to download. Download the latest version of JDK as per your OS and system requirements.

Download and Install JDK in order to create Android Application Source Files using the Java or Kotlin Programming Language. The system will execute the code using a set of Libraries and Compilers.

Steps to Install JDK on Windows:

Step 1: Download the latest Oracle Java Development Kit (JDK) from the Official Oracle Website (https://www.oracle.com/java/technologies/downloads/) as per your system specifications.

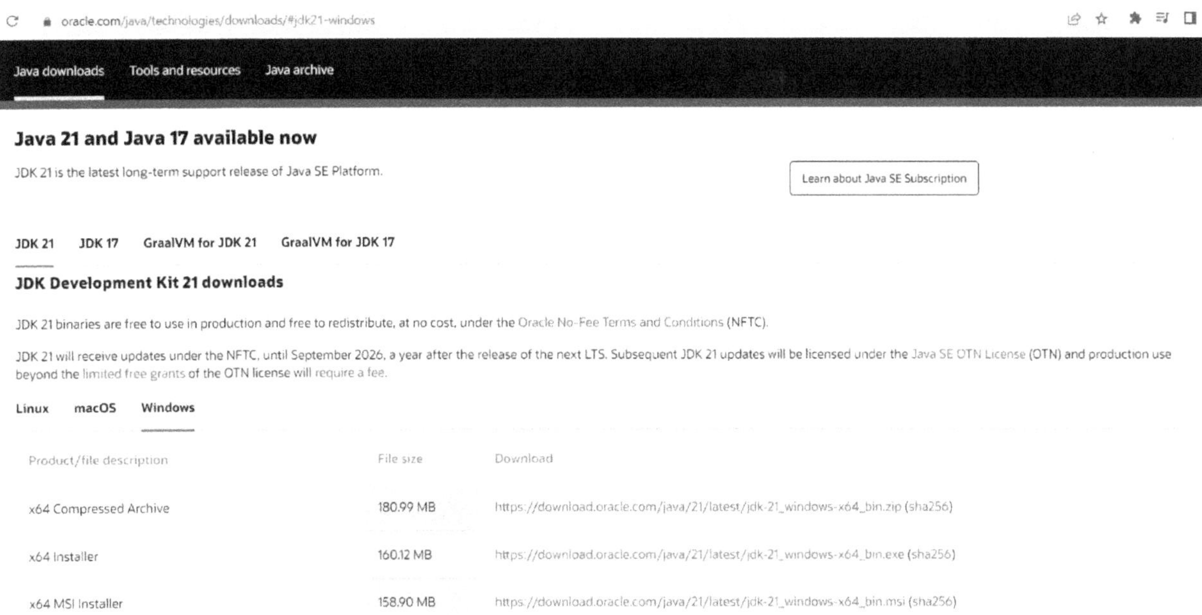

Step 2: After the download is complete, proceed to install the JDK. Double-click on the application downloaded to see the start of the installation process. Now click on the Next button to proceed.

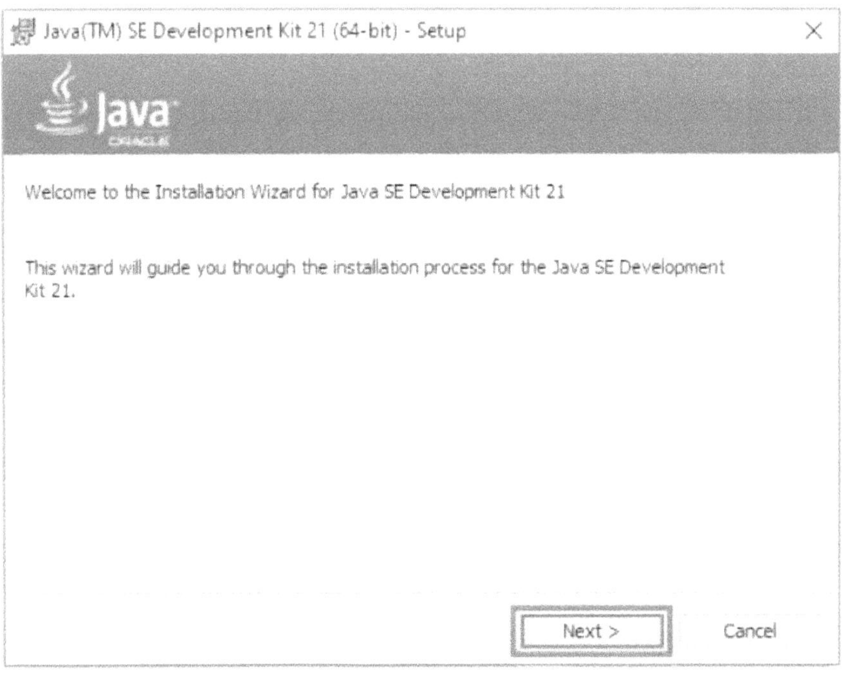

Step 3: Now, here you have a choice to change the Java installation directory by clicking on the **Change** button otherwise simply go with the default path by clicking the **Next** button. We will go with the default path only.

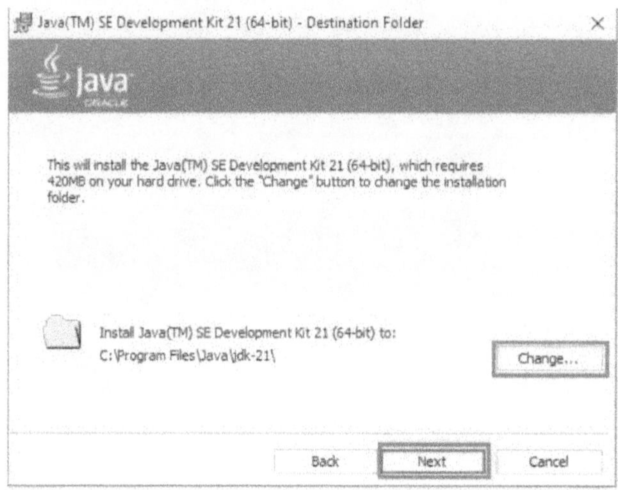

Once you click the Next button, you will see the start of the installation process as below image.

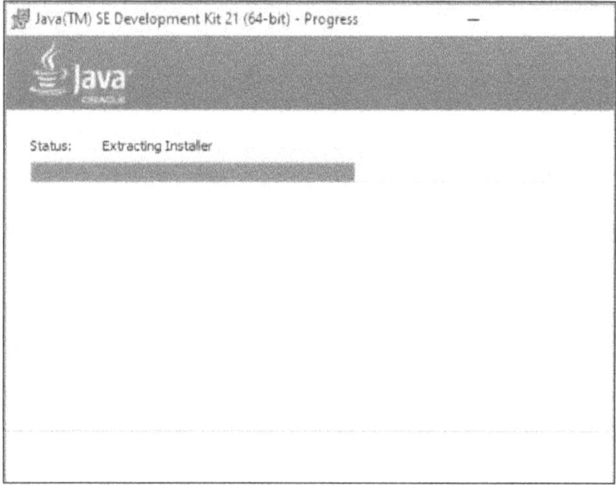

After successful installation, Click on **Close** button to close the installation wizard.

Step 4: Open the system environment variables dialog to do the setup. To open the dialog, type "System environment" in the Window's search box as below image and open it.

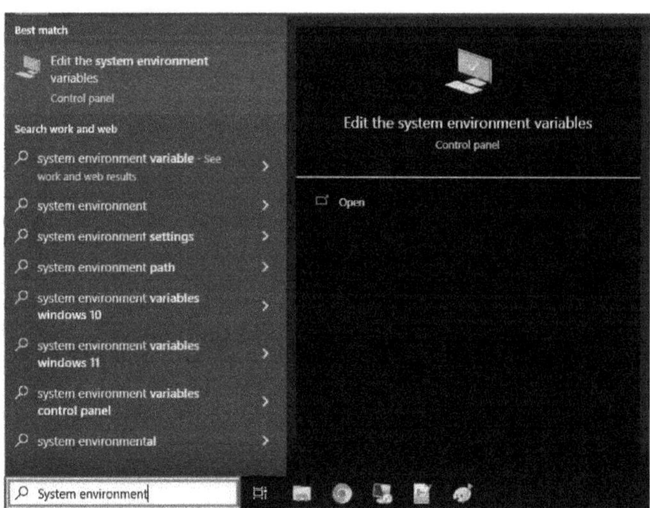

Once it's open you can able to see the below dialog box.

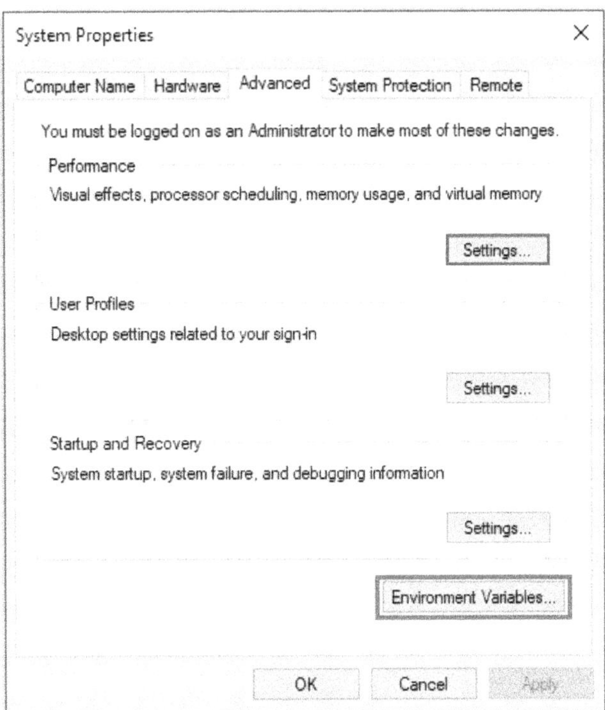

Step 5: Now click on the Environment Variables button > add JAVA_HOME & edit Path as shown in the below images:

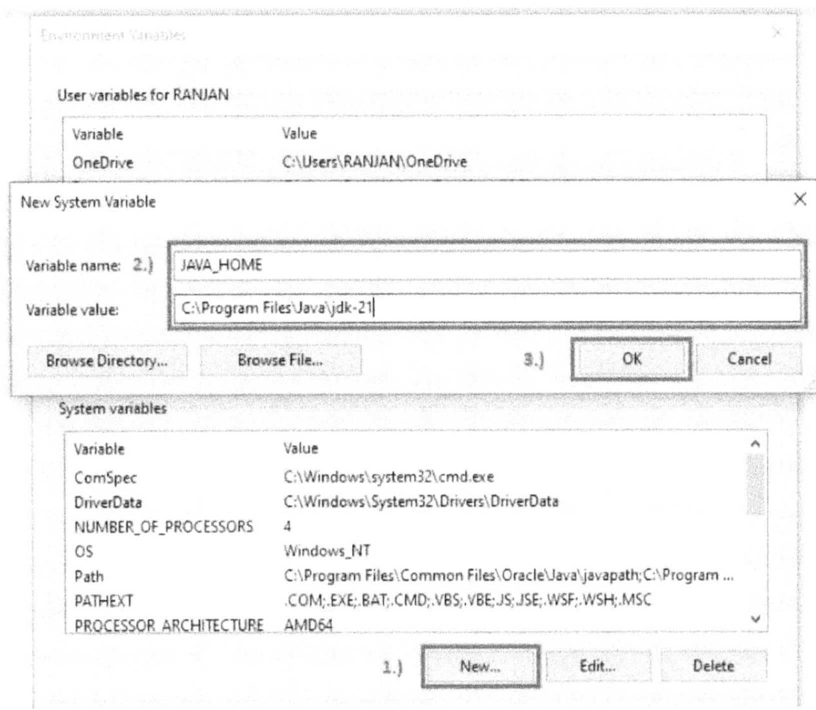

Step 5: Now we have to add Java Path. If the Path variable is already there, then simply we click on the Edit button, then click the New button to add the path as below image.

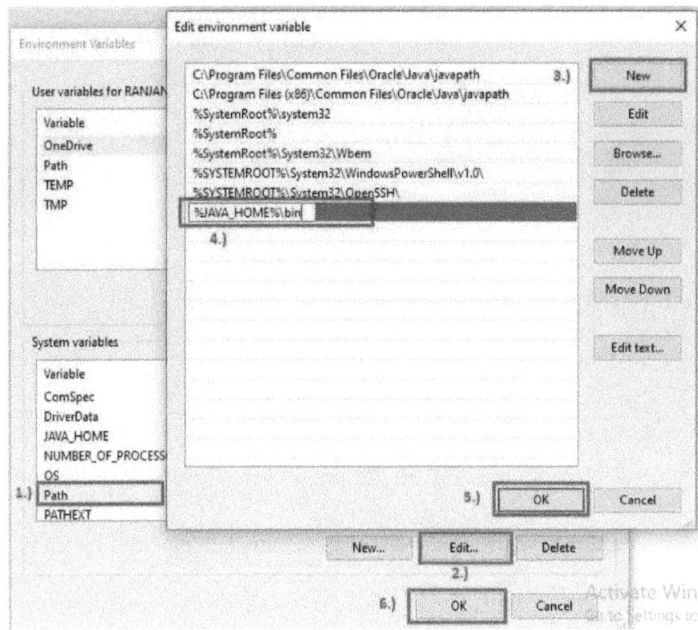

Step 7: (Check the Java Version) Open Command Prompt and enter the following commands:

```
java -version
javac -version
```

```
Command Prompt
Microsoft Windows [Version 10.0.22000.675]
(c) Microsoft Corporation. All rights reserved.

C:\Users\sarth>java -version
java version "18.0.1.1" 2022-04-22
Java(TM) SE Runtime Environment (build 18.0.1.1+2-6)
Java HotSpot(TM) 64-Bit Server VM (build 18.0.1.1+2-6, mixed mode, sharing)

C:\Users\sarth>javac -version
javac 18.0.1.1

C:\Users\sarth>
```

Steps to Install JDK on Linux:

Step 1: Download and Install Oracle Java Development Kit (JDK). To install the downloaded JDK File using terminal, Open terminal and change your directory to downloads by using the command:

```
$ cd downloads
```

To list files and packages present in the directory, Type

```
$ ls
```

Step 2: Now we use Debian Package Manager to configure our downloaded file for installation by typing

```
$ sudo dpkg -i jdk-{YOUR_JDK_VERSION}          (replace {-} with your version)
```

Enter your password

Step 3: Now, type the following commands to proceed with the installation

```
$ sudo update-alternatives --install /usr/bin/java java /usr/lib/jvm/jdk-
{YOUR_JDK_VERSION}/bin/java 1

$ sudo update-alternatives --install /usr/bin/javac javac /usr/lib/jvm/jdk-
{YOUR_JDK_VERSION}/bin/javac 1
```

Step 4: (Check the Java Version) Open the terminal and enter the following commands

```
$ java --version

$ javac --version
```

Step 5: (Configure JAVA_HOME Environment Variable) After the installation is complete, we have to configure environment variables to notify the system about the directory in which jdk files are located. To find the Location of the JDK Files, run this command

```
$ sudo update-alternatives --config java
```

and copy the File Location.

Step 6: In order to set the environment variable, you have to edit the environment file using this command

```
$ sudo gedit /etc/environment
```

Proceed to add JAVA_HOME=" /usr/lib/jvm/jdk-{YOUR_JDK_VERSION}"

Then, save and close the file.

Step 7: Now, refresh the environment file by using this command

```
$ SOURCE /etc/environment
```

And echo the JAVA_HOME Path

```
$ echo $JAVA_HOME
```


Steps to Install JDK on Mac OS:

Step 1: Download the Oracle Java Development Kit (JDK) from the Official Oracle Website.

Step 2: After the download is complete, proceed to install the JDK by following the bootstrapped steps.

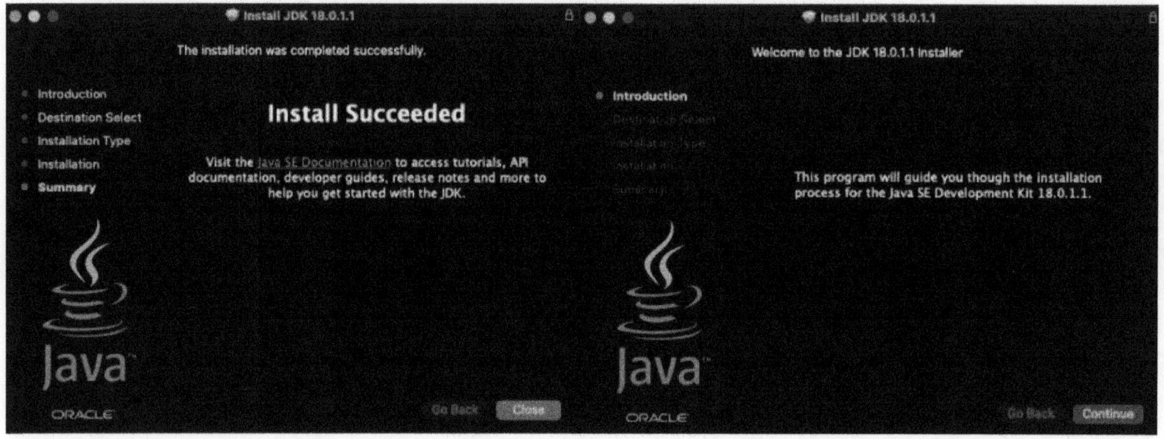

Step 3: (Configure environment variables) Now to configure, open the terminal and pass the following commands. To find the Location of the JAVA_HOME, run this command

```
$ /usr/libexec/java_home -v{YOUR_VERSION}
```

Step 4: Set this output as our JAVA_HOME Environment Variable. You can use any command or code editor to edit the file,

```
$ code ~/. bash_profile
```

Step 5: Export the path we obtained earlier i.e.

```
$export  JAVA_HOME=/Library/Java/JavaVirtualMachines/jdk-{YOUR_VERSION}.jdk/
Contents/Home
```

Step 6: Refresh the environment file by using this command

```
$ source ~/.bash_profile
```

And echo the JAVA_HOME variable

```
$ echo $JAVA_HOME
```

Step 7: (Check the Java Version) In the terminal, enter the following commands

```
$ java -version
```

```
$ javac -version
```

Installing Android Studio

Android Studio is the official IDE (Integrated Development Environment) for Android app development and it is based on JetBrains' IntelliJ IDEA software. Android Studio provides many excellent features that enhance productivity when building Android apps, such as:

- A blended environment where one can develop for all Android devices
- Apply Changes to push code and resource changes to the running app without restarting the app

- A flexible Gradle-based build system
- A fast and feature-rich emulator
- GitHub and Code template integration to assist you to develop common app features and import sample code
- Extensive testing tools and frameworks
- C++ and NDK support
- Built-in support for Google Cloud Platform, making it easy to integrate Google Cloud Messaging and App Engine, and many more.
- Provides GUI tools that simplify the less interesting parts of app development.
- Easy integration with real time database 'firebase'.

System Requirements

- Microsoft Windows 7/8/10/11 (32-bit or 64-bit)
- 4 GB RAM minimum, 8 GB RAM recommended (plus 1 GB for the Android Emulator)
- 2 GB of available disk space minimum, 4 GB recommended (500 MB for IDE plus 1.5 GB for Android SDK and emulator system image)
- 1280 x 800 minimum screen resolution

Installation

Step 1: Go to Android Developer site (https://developer.android.com/studio#downloads) and click on ***Download Android Studio*** button

Step 2: Open the downloaded file to install Android Studio.

Step 3: An Installation Dialog box will appear. Click on Next.

Step 4: Choose a path for installation and click on Next. Installation will start.

Step 5: Once the installation in complete, click on Next, then click on Finish.

Step 6: Android Studio will be started. Meanwhile it will be finding the SDK components.

Finding Available SDK Components

Downloading...

https://dl.google.com/android/repository/repository2-1.xml

Step 7: After it has found the SDK components, it will redirect to the Welcome dialog box.

Step 8: Choose Install type as Standard and click on Next.

Step 9: Now it is time to download the SDK components.

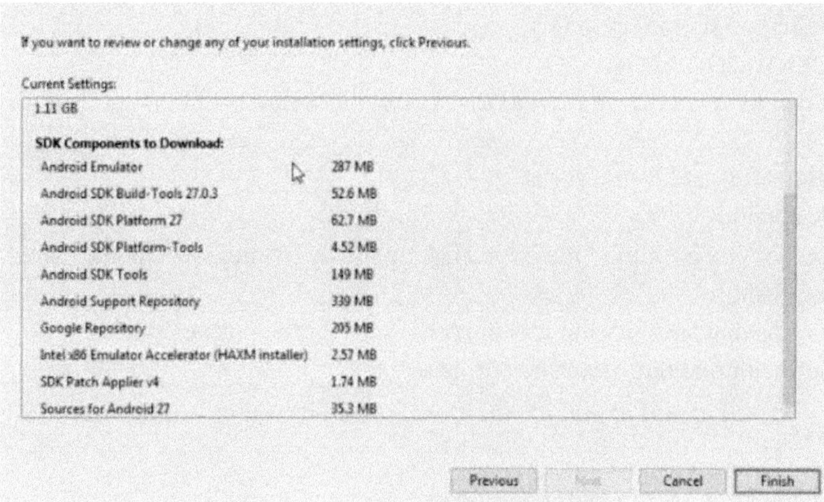

Step 10: Click on Finish. Components begin to download let it complete.

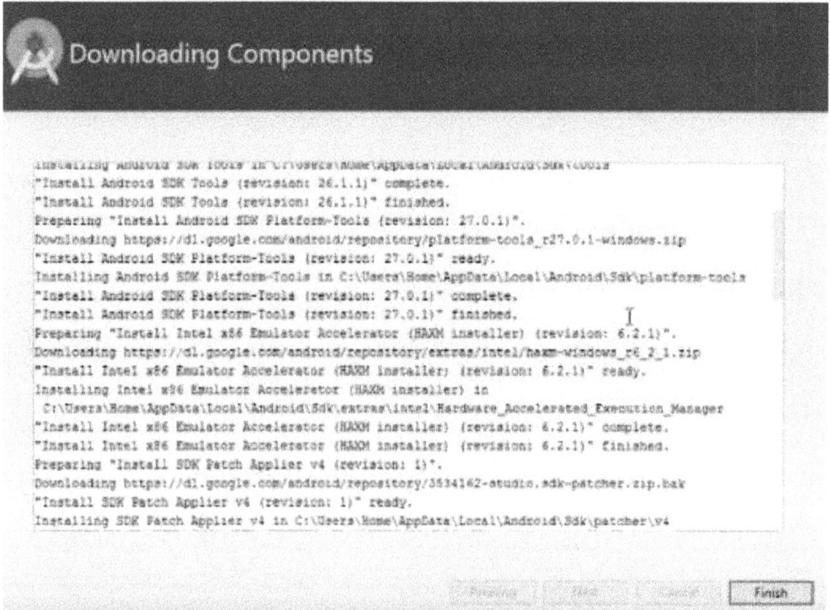

Step 11: The Android Studio has been successfully configured. Now it's time to launch and build apps. Click on the Finish button to launch it.

Step 12: Click on Start a new Android Studio project to build a new app.

Setting up an Android Project

After successfully installing the Android studio and opening it for the first time, below are the steps to start and set up a new android project in Android Studio:

1. Select the *Start a new Android Studio Project* option to start a new android project.
2. In the New Project screen that appears, you can select the type of project you want to create from categories of device form factors, shown in the Templates pane. For example, below figure shows the project templates for phone and tablet.

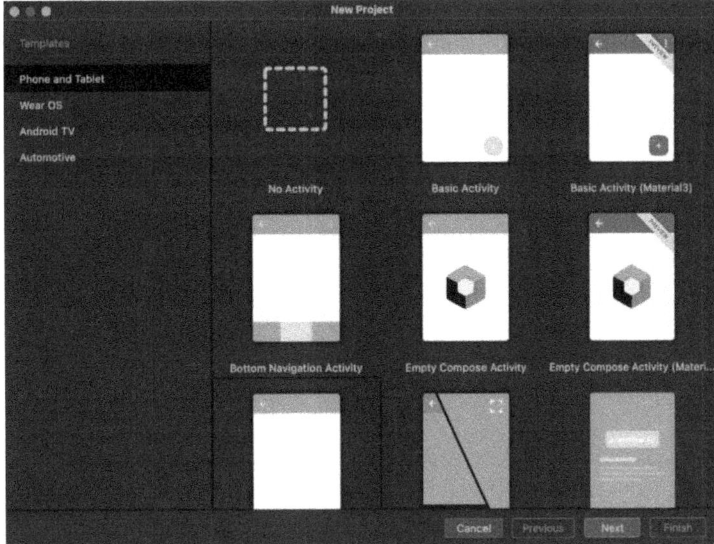

Selecting the type of project you want to create lets Android Studio include sample code and resources in your project to help you get started.

3. Once you select your project type, click Next.
4. The next step in creating your project is to configure some settings, as shown in below figure.

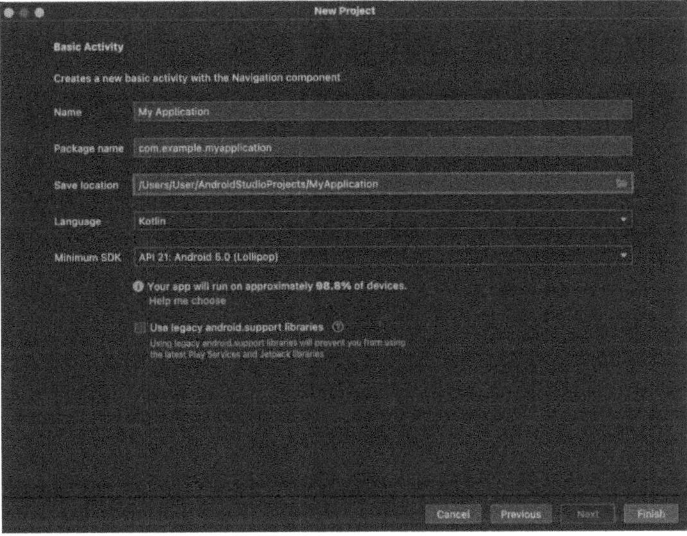

5. Specify the Name of your project.
6. Specify the Package name. By default, this package name becomes your project's namespace (used to access your project resources) and your project's application ID (used as the ID for publishing).
7. Specify the Save location where you want to locally store your project.
8. Select the Language, Kotlin or Java, you want Android Studio to use when creating sample code for your new project. Keep in mind that you aren't limited to using only that language in the project.
9. Select the Minimum API level you want your app to support. When you select a lower API level, your app can't use as many modern Android APIs. However, a larger percentage of Android devices can run your app. The opposite is true when selecting a higher API level.
10. Click on Finish, your project will be created.

Build your First App – Hello World

After successfully setting up an Android project, all of the default files are created with default code in them. Let us look at this default code and files and try to run the default app created.

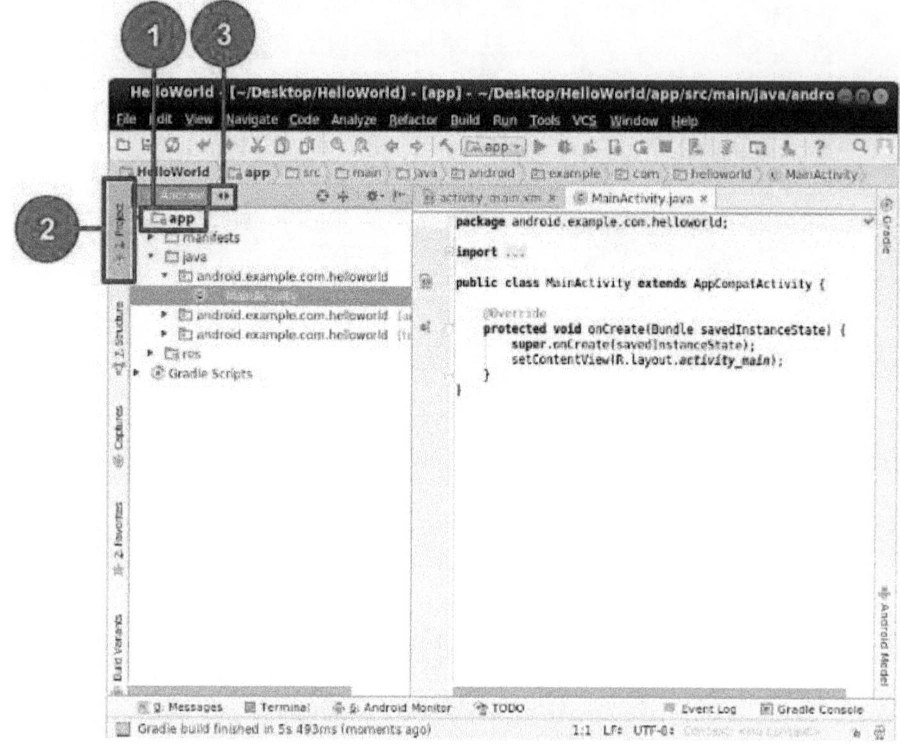

Look at the hierarchy of the files for your app in multiple ways.

  i.   Click on the Hello World folder to expand the hierarchy of files (1),
  ii.   Click on Project (2).
  iii. Click on the Android menu (3).
  iv.   Explore the different view options for your project.

- The panel on the left side of the android studio window has all the files that the app includes. Under the java folder, observe the first folder containing the java file of your project.
- For every activity, a ".java" file and a ".xml" file is created. In this case for MainActivity, "MainActivity.java" and "activity_main.xml" are created.
- The above java file shows us the default code that is present when an app is created. An activity is created that extends AppCompactActivity class.
- The "res" folder contains "layout" subfolder, which includes the xml files of the projects.
- You can find the activity_main.xml file under the layout folder. This the XML file corresponding to the MainActivity. There is an onCreate function that overrides a function of AppCompactActivity class. onCreate(Bundle) is where you initialize your activity. When the activity is first started, then both onCreate() methods are called. But after the first start of Activity, the onCreate() of application will not be called for subsequent runs.
- Now, consider the activity_main.xml file, it contains various tags similar to HTML. The first tag ensures the version. The second tag is usually the Layout tag. There are various types of Layouts but for now, let us go with the default RelativeLayout. This is a layout that places the widgets relative to screen size.

- There is a TextView widget by default. This "TextView" is basically the Text field that displays the text specified. It has various attributes. For now, consider the default attributes present. The layout_width and layout_height are the width and height of the widget occupied in the screen. The attribute "wrap_content" refers to width or height being restricted to the content of the text.
- The text attribute takes a string in quotations (i.e., " "). The content within this is displayed on the screen.
- Type *Hello World* in the quotations.

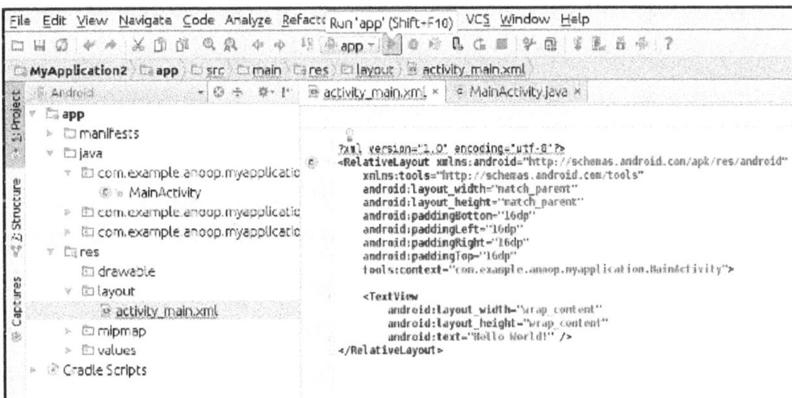

- Now, click the "Run" option at the Toolbar at the top.

Note: You can either choose the emulator or you can connect your phone and find them listed under Connected Devices but for this you must enable the developer options in your phone and set the USB debugging mode on.

This is how your first app would like.

With this, congratulations on developing your first app!

PART 2

Getting Through Android Studio

CHAPTER 3

OVERVIEW OF ANDROID STUDIO

A ndroid Studio is the official integrated development environment (IDE) for Android application development. It is based on IntelliJ IDEA, a Java integrated development environment for software, and incorporates its code editing and developer tools.

To support application development within the Android operating system, Android Studio uses a Gradle-based build system, Android Emulator, code templates and GitHub integration. Every project in Android Studio has one or more modalities with source code and resource files. These modalities include Android app modules, Library modules and Google App Engine modules.

Android Studio uses an Apply Changes feature to push code and resource changes to a running application. A code editor assists the developer with writing code and offering code completion, refraction and analysis. Applications built in Android Studio are then compiled into the APK format for submission to the Google Play Store.

The software was first announced at Google I/O in May 2013, and the first stable build was released in December 2014. Android Studio is available for macOS, Windows and Linux desktop platforms. It replaced Eclipse Android Development Tools (ADT) as the primary IDE for Android application development.

After many releases of ADT plugin for Eclipse, Google decided to build its own IDE for Android Application Development. In December, 2014 Google released its first stable build of Android Studio v1.0. Before this, Google had already give early access to preview stage Android Studio v0.1 for the developers in May, 2013 and later in June, 2014 they released beta stage starting from v0.8.

Features of Android Studio

Android Studio is the official integrated development environment (IDE) for Android app development. It offers a wide range of features and tools that make it easier for developers to create, test, and deploy Android applications. Here are some of the key features of Android Studio:

1. **User Interface (UI) Designer:** Android Studio includes a powerful UI designer that allows developers to visually create and modify the user interface of their Android apps. It supports drag-and-drop functionality for building layouts and offers a preview mode to see how the UI will appear on different devices.
2. **Code Editor:** Android Studio features a code editor with intelligent code completion, code analysis, and error checking. It supports multiple programming languages, including Java and Kotlin.
3. **Gradle Build System:** Android Studio uses the Gradle build system to automate the build and deployment process. This makes it easy to manage dependencies, build variants, and generate APKs for different device configurations.
4. **Emulator:** Android Studio includes an Android Emulator that allows developers to test their apps on various virtual Android devices with different screen sizes, resolutions, and Android versions.
5. **Debugging Tools:** Android Studio provides robust debugging tools, including breakpoints, variable inspection, and real-time code analysis to help developers find and fix bugs in their code.
6. **Profiling and Performance Analysis:** Developers can use the built-in profiling tools to monitor the performance of their apps, identify bottlenecks, and optimize resource usage.

7. **Version Control Integration:** Android Studio integrates with popular version control systems like Git, making it easy for developers to manage and collaborate on code with their team.
8. **Layout Inspector:** This tool allows developers to inspect the layout hierarchy of their app's user interface and view properties at runtime, which can be helpful for diagnosing UI issues.
9. **APK Analyzer:** Developers can use the APK Analyzer to examine the contents and structure of APK files, helping to reduce the size of the app and optimize resource usage.
10. **Templates and Wizards:** Android Studio provides templates and wizards to quickly create common components such as activities, fragments, and app navigation.
11. **Android Virtual Device (AVD) Manager:** This tool allows developers to create and manage Android Virtual Devices for testing and debugging, with control over various device configurations.
12. **Instant Run:** Android Studio supports Instant Run, which allows developers to see code changes in their app without the need for a full rebuild and redeployment.
13. **Code Templates and Snippets:** Android Studio provides code templates and snippets to streamline common coding tasks and promote best practices.
14. **Localization Tools:** Developers can manage and test app translations and string resources easily with Android Studio's localization tools.
15. **Data Binding:** Android Studio supports data binding, which simplifies the connection between the UI and the underlying data model in Android apps.
16. **Kotlin Support:** Android Studio has excellent support for the Kotlin programming language, making it easier for developers to write Android apps using Kotlin.
17. **Android Jetpack:** Android Studio integrates with Android Jetpack, a set of libraries and tools that helps developers build high-quality Android apps more quickly and easily.

These are just some of the many features offered by Android Studio, making it a comprehensive and powerful IDE for Android app development.

Project Package Structure

In the previous chapter, we learned how to setup Android Studio and how to create our first Android Application and how to run it. When we create an android project, Android Studio generates the application project with a few default packages and folders. Here, in this topic we'll discuss about the project structure of an Android Application.

In Android Studio, the package structure is an essential part of organizing your Android app's source code and resources. It helps maintain a logical and structured organization for your project. Here's a typical package structure you might find in an Android project:

1. **Java/Kotlin Source Code Packages:**
    a. **app/src/main/java:** This is where your primary source code resides. It's organized based on the Java or Kotlin package structure. Typically, it includes packages for different components and features of your app.
       Example:
    o   com.example.myapp: The root package.
    o   com.example.myapp.activities: Contains your app's activity classes.
    o   com.example.myapp.fragments: Contains your app's fragment classes.
    o   com.example.myapp.adapters: Contains custom adapters.
    o   com.example.myapp.utils: Contains utility classes.
2. **Resources:**
    a. **app/src/main/res:** This directory holds various resources used in your app. It's further organized into subdirectories based on resource type and configuration. Subdirectories include:

o   drawable: For image resources.
o   layout: XML layout files for your app's UI.
o   values: XML files for strings, colors, dimensions, and other resources.
o   mipmap: For launcher icons.
o   menu: XML files for app menus.
o   anim: XML files for animations.
o   raw: For raw asset files.
o   xml: For XML files other than layouts.

3. **Manifest:**
    a. **app/src/main:** The AndroidManifest.xml file resides here. It defines your app's configuration, permissions, and components.

4. **Test Packages:**
    a. **app/src/androidTest/java:** Contains instrumentation tests for your app.
    b. **app/src/test/java:** Houses unit tests for your app.

5. **Gradle Scripts:**
    a. **app:** This directory contains Gradle build scripts for your app, such as build.gradle and proguard-rules.pro.

6. **Libraries and Modules:**

If you have additional libraries or modules in your project, they may have their own package structure within their respective directories.

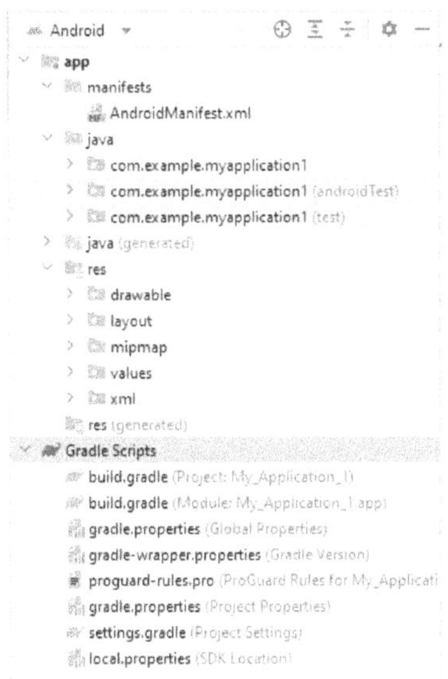

(Fig. 3.1: Android Studio Project Structure)

Introduction to Gradle

In Android Studio, Gradle is used for building our android application projects, hence playing the role of a build system. Every android application development tool has to compile resources, java source code, external libraries and combine them into a final APK.

Gradle is a build system, which is responsible for code compilation, testing, deployment and conversion of the code into .dex files and hence running the app on the device.

As Android Studio comes with Gradle system pre-installed, there is no need to install additional runtime software(s) to build our project. Whenever you click on Run button in android studio, a gradle task automatically triggers and starts building the project and after gradle completes its task, app starts running in AVD or in the connected device.

A build system like Gradle is not a compiler, linker etc, but it controls and supervises the operation of compilation, linking of files, running test cases, and eventually bundling the code into an apk file for your Android Application.

There are two build.gradle files for every android studio project of which, one is for application and other is for project level (module level) build files.

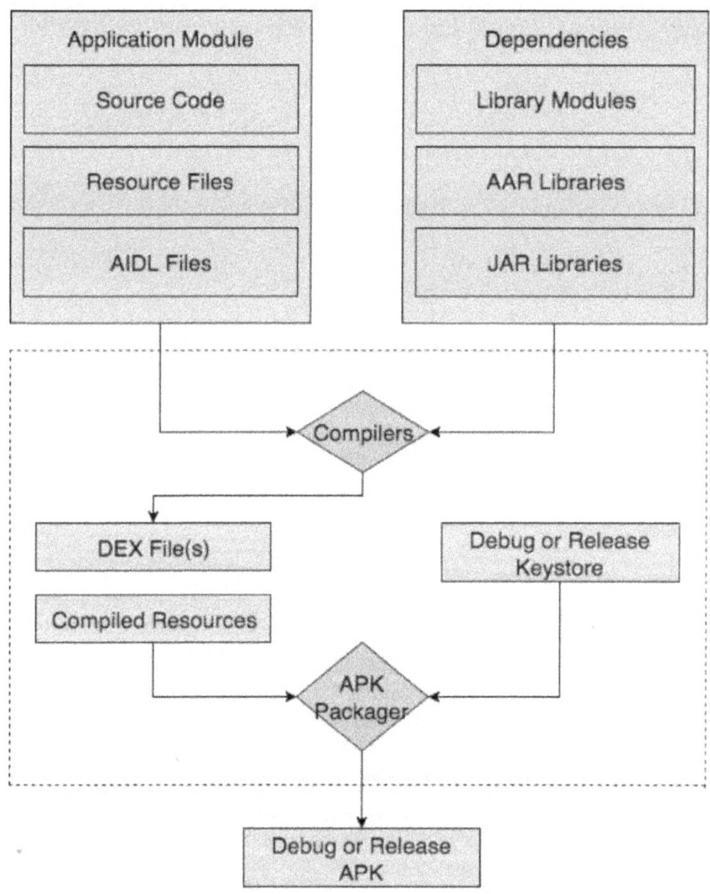

(Fig, 3.2) Gradle build process

In the build process, the compiler takes the source code, resources, external libraries JAR files and AndroidManifest.xml(which contains the meta-data about the application) and convert them into .dex (Dalvik Executable files) files, which includes bytecode. That bytecode is supported by all android devices to run your app. Then APK Manager combines the .dex files and all other resources into single apk file. APK Packager signs debug or release apk using respective debug or release keystore.

Debug apk is generally used for testing purpose or we can say that it is used at development stage only. When your app is complete with desired features and you are ready to publish your application for external use then you require a Release apk signed using a release keystore.

Now let's shed some light on the gradle files.

- **setting.gradle:** The setting.gradle (Gradle setting) file is used to specify all the modules used in your app.
- **build.gradle (project level):** The Top level (module) build.gradle file is project level build file, which defines build configurations at project level. This file applies configurations to all the modules in android application project.
- **build.gradle (application level):** The Application level build.gradle file is located in each module of the android project. This file includes your package name as applicationID, version name (apk version), version code, minimum and target sdk for a specific application module. When you are including external libraries (not the jar files) then you need to mention it in the app level gradle file to include them in your project as dependencies of the application.

Android Virtual Device (AVD)

An Android Virtual Device (AVD) is a device configuration that runs on the Android Emulator. It provides virtual device-specific Android Environment in which we can install & test our Android Application. AVD Manager is a part of SDK Manager to create and manage the virtual devices created.

To open AVD manager, go to Tools → Android → AVD Manager as shown in below image.

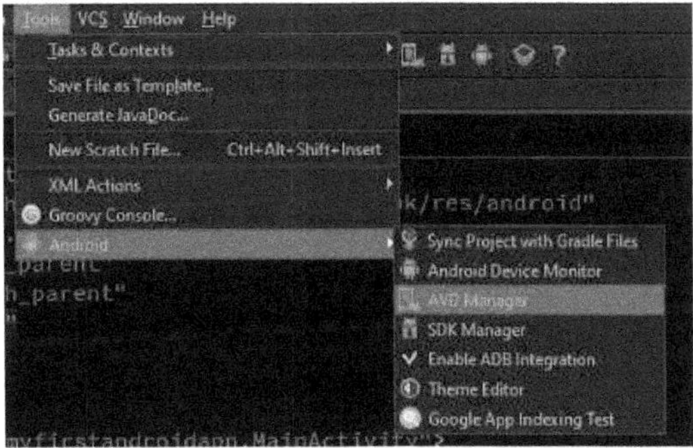

It will open AVD Manager with a list of created virtual devices as shown in below image. It may be empty for you now as you haven't created any device as of now. To create a new device, click on Create Virtual Device button.

Below procedure can be followed step-by-step to create a new Virtual Device:

1. Open the Device Manager.
2. Click Create Device. (The Select Hardware window appears.)

3. Select a hardware profile, then click Next.

(If you don't see the hardware profile you want, you can create or import a hardware profile, as described in other sections on this page.) The System Image window appears.

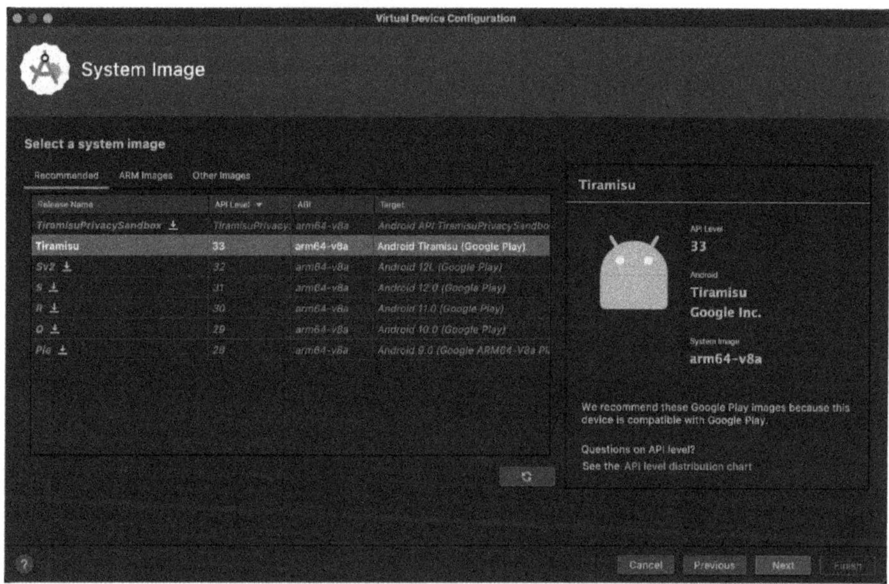

4. Select the system image for a particular API level, and then click Next. (The Verify Configuration window appears.)
5. Change the AVD properties as needed, and then click Finish.

The new AVD appears in the Virtual tab of the Device Manager and the target device menu.

Android Layouts

In Android app development, layouts are used to define the structure and appearance of the user interface (UI) of an app. Layouts determine how UI elements, such as buttons, text views, and images, are arranged and displayed on the screen. Android provides several types of layout classes to achieve different UI designs. Here are some commonly used Android layouts:

1. LinearLayout

- LinearLayout arranges child views in a single row or column, either horizontally or vertically.
- You can specify the distribution of space among child views using layout weights.
- It's a simple and lightweight layout, suitable for creating basic UI structures.

Example XML:

```xml
<LinearLayout
    android:layout_width="match_parent"
    android:layout_height="wrap_content"
    android:orientation="vertical">
    <Button
        android:layout_width="match_parent"
        android:layout_height="wrap_content"
        android:text="Button 1" />
    <Button
        android:layout_width="match_parent"
        android:layout_height="wrap_content"
        android:text="Button 2" />
</LinearLayout>
```

2. RelativeLayout

- RelativeLayout allows you to position child views relative to each other or to the parent view.
- You can define rules for positioning elements, such as aligning to the parent's edges or other views.
- It's versatile for creating complex UIs with specific positioning requirements.

Example XML:

```xml
<RelativeLayout
    android:layout_width="match_parent"
    android:layout_height="match_parent">
```

```xml
    <Button

        android:id="@+id/button1"

        android:layout_width="wrap_content"

        android:layout_height="wrap_content"

        android:text="Button 1"

        android:layout_alignParentTop="true"

        android:layout_alignParentStart="true" />

    <Button

        android:layout_width="wrap_content"

        android:layout_height="wrap_content"

        android:text="Button 2"

        android:layout_below="@id/button1"

        android:layout_toEndOf="@id/button1" />

</RelativeLayout>
```

3. ConstraintLayout

- ConstraintLayout is a flexible layout that uses constraints to define the position and size of UI elements.
- It's suitable for creating responsive designs that adapt to various screen sizes and orientations.
- Constraints can be set to other views, guidelines, or parent edges, offering fine-grained control.

Example XML:

```xml
<androidx.constraintlayout.widget.ConstraintLayout

    android:layout_width="match_parent"

    android:layout_height="match_parent">

    <Button

        android:id="@+id/button1"

        android:layout_width="wrap_content"

        android:layout_height="wrap_content"

        android:text="Button 1"

        app:layout_constraintTop_toTopOf="parent"

        app:layout_constraintStart_toStartOf="parent" />
```

```xml
<Button

    android:layout_width="wrap_content"

    android:layout_height="wrap_content"

    android:text="Button 2"

    app:layout_constraintTop_toBottomOf="@id/button1"

    app:layout_constraintStart_toEndOf="@id/button1" />

</androidx.constraintlayout.widget.ConstraintLayout>
```

4. FrameLayout

- FrameLayout is a simple layout that places child views on top of each other, with the last child added appearing at the top.
- It's often used for displaying a single view as the primary content, such as fragments or images.

Example XML:

```xml
<FrameLayout

    android:layout_width="match_parent"

    android:layout_height="match_parent">

    <ImageView

        android:layout_width="match_parent"

        android:layout_height="match_parent"

        android:src="@drawable/image" />

    <TextView

        android:layout_width="wrap_content"

        android:layout_height="wrap_content"

        android:text="Overlay Text"

        android:layout_gravity="center" />

</FrameLayout>
```

5. GridLayout

- GridLayout arranges child views in a grid, similar to a table, with rows and columns.
- It's suitable for creating UIs with a consistent grid-like structure, such as calculator apps.

Example XML:

```xml
<GridLayout
```

```xml
    android:layout_width="match_parent"

    android:layout_height="wrap_content"

    android:columnCount="2">

    <Button

        android:layout_width="wrap_content"

        android:layout_height="wrap_content"

        android:text="Button 1" />

    <Button

        android:layout_width="wrap_content"

        android:layout_height="wrap_content"

        android:text="Button 2" />

    <!-- Add more buttons here -->

</GridLayout>
```

6. TableLayout

- TableLayout is used to create a table-like structure, where child views are organized in rows and columns.
- It's suitable for presenting data in tabular form.

Example XML:

```xml
<TableLayout

    android:layout_width="match_parent"

    android:layout_height="wrap_content">

    <TableRow>

        <TextView

            android:layout_width="wrap_content"

            android:layout_height="wrap_content"

            android:text="Name" />

        <TextView

            android:layout_width="wrap_content"

            android:layout_height="wrap_content"

            android:text="Age" />
```

```xml
        </TableRow>

        <TableRow>

            <TextView

                android:layout_width="wrap_content"

                android:layout_height="wrap_content"

                android:text="John" />

            <TextView

                android:layout_width="wrap_content"

                android:layout_height="wrap_content"

                android:text="25" />

        </TableRow>

        <!-- Add more rows here -->

</TableLayout>
```

7. ScrollView:

- ScrollView is not a layout in itself but is often used to wrap other layouts or views to enable scrolling when the content doesn't fit within the available screen space.
- This is useful for long lists or text content.

Example XML:

```xml
<ScrollView

    android:layout_width="match_parent"

    android:layout_height="match_parent">

    <LinearLayout

        android:layout_width="match_parent"

        android:layout_height="wrap_content"

        android:orientation="vertical">

        <!-- Content that exceeds screen size -->

    </LinearLayout>

</ScrollView>
```

8. CoordinatorLayout:

- CoordinatorLayout is used for creating complex UI interactions and animations, often in combination with the Android Design Support Library.
- It allows for controlling the behavior of child views in response to various events and gestures.

Example XML:

```xml
<androidx.coordinatorlayout.widget.CoordinatorLayout

    android:layout_width="match_parent"

    android:layout_height="match_parent">

    <AppBarLayout

        android:layout_width="match_parent"

        android:layout_height="wrap_content">

        <!-- App bar content -->

    </AppBarLayout>

    <NestedScrollView

        android:layout_width="match_parent"

        android:layout_height="match_parent">

        <!-- Scrollable content -->

    </NestedScrollView>

</androidx.coordinatorlayout.widget.CoordinatorLayout>
```

These are some of the commonly used Android layouts, and you can combine them and nest them to create complex and responsive user interfaces for your Android apps. The choice of layout depends on your app's design requirements and the specific arrangement of UI elements you need to achieve.

Android Views & Widget

View is the basic building block of UI (User Interface) in android. View refers to the android.view.View class, which is the super class for all the GUI components like TextView, ImageView, Button, etc.

View class extends Object class and implements Drawable.Callback, KeyEvent.Callback and AccessibilityEvent Source.

View can be considered as a rectangle on the screen that shows some type of content. It can be an image, a piece of text, a button or anything that an android application can display. The rectangle here is actually invisible, but every view occupies a rectangle shape.

The rectangle can be resized by specifying the exact size (with proper units) or by using some predefined values. These predefined values are *match_parent* and *wrap_content*.

- *match_parent* means it will occupy the complete space available on the display of the device.
- Whereas, *wrap_content* means it will occupy only that much space as required for its content to display.

A View is also known as Widget in Android. Any visual (that we can see on screen) and interactive (with which user can interact with) is called a Widget.

Activities in Android

- The Activity class is a crucial component of an Android app, and the way activities are launched and put together is a fundamental part of the platform's application model.
- Unlike programming paradigms in which apps are launched with a main() method, the Android system initiates code in an Activity instance by invoking specific callback methods that correspond to specific stages of its lifecycle.
- Activity is nothing but a java class in Android which has some pre-defined functions which are triggered at different App states, which we can override to perform anything we want.
- Activity class provides us with empty functions allowing us to be the controller of everything.
- An activity is the entry point for interacting with the user. Every activity contains the layout, which has a user interface to interact with the user.

Let's understand this with a real life example,

The human mind holds sway over our emotions, thoughts, and responses, triggering sensations of pain in the face of physical or emotional injury, evoking tears or laughter in response to stimuli. Our real-world experiences, such as physical harm or sensory input, are processed and understood by our mind, whether it be the conscious or the soul, shaping our thoughts and actions accordingly.

In a similar vein, one could analogize our body as a mere physical entity, with our mind (soul or consciousness) serving as the driving force dictating our responses to various situations.

Drawing a parallel to Android development, the user interface - comprising Views, Layouts, and ViewGroups - constitutes the tangible appearance of our app. In this analogy, the mind or soul of our app would be represented by the **Activity**.

As an example, consider a function dictated by our mind, let's call it `onSeeingSomethingFunny()`. While we may be aware of its default behavior, it becomes intriguing when we have the ability to override and furnish our own definition for this function.

```
@Override

void onSeeingSomethingFunny() {

    startCrying();

}
```

In this scenario, we've overridden the default behavior, and instead of the expected response to something funny, the function now initiates the action of crying. This concept illustrates the capacity to customize and redefine our reactions based on our own preferences or circumstances.

- One notable distinction between the human context and our example lies in the life cycle. A human is brought into existence at birth, undergoes various experiences throughout life, and ultimately ceases to exist at death. Throughout this journey, the mind/soul/consciousness guides and influences actions.

  In contrast, an Activity in the context of Android is responsible not only for controlling the app but also for managing its life cycle, encompassing creation, destruction, and various states. An app's life cycle can iterate infinitely, with Activities playing a crucial role in this process.

  While multiple Activities can exist in an Android app, there is typically one designated as the Main Activity. Analogously, in languages like Java, C, or C++, program execution begins with the `main()` method. Similarly, when a user initiates the app by clicking its icon, the Main Activity is invoked, and the execution commences from the `onCreate()` method of the Activity class.

Managing the Activity Lifecycle:

Throughout its lifespan, an activity undergoes various states, and the navigation between these states is managed through a series of callbacks. The following sections introduce these crucial callbacks.

1. **onCreate():**

- This callback is imperative, and its implementation is mandatory. It is triggered when the system initiates the creation of your activity.
- During this phase, your code should initialize the fundamental components of your activity. For instance, creating views and binding data to lists should occur here. Most notably, this is the juncture where you must invoke setContentView() to articulate the layout for the activity's user interface.
- Upon the completion of onCreate(), the subsequent callback in the sequence is consistently onStart().

2. **onStart():**

- Upon the exit of onCreate(), the activity transitions into the Started state, becoming visible to the user. This callback encapsulates the final preparations for the activity's foreground appearance and user interaction.

3. **onResume():**
- Invoked just before the activity engages with the user, onResume() marks the activity as the topmost element in the activity stack, capturing all user input.
- This method typically houses the core functionality of an app. Following onResume(), the onPause() callback is invariably invoked.

4. **onPause():**

- Triggered when the activity loses focus and enters a Paused state, onPause() is called when the user interacts with navigation buttons, like Back or Recents. Although the activity remains partially visible, this often signifies the user's departure from the activity.
- An activity in the Paused state can continue updating the UI based on user expectations.
- It is not recommended for tasks such as saving data, making network calls, or executing database transactions.
- The next callbacks after onPause() are either onStop() or onResume(), contingent on the subsequent state after entering the Paused state.

5. onStop():

- Invoked when the activity is no longer visible to the user, onStop() may occur due to the activity being destroyed, a new activity starting, or an existing activity entering a Resumed state. At this point, the activity is entirely invisible.
- Subsequent callbacks are either onRestart() if the activity is resuming interaction or onDestroy() if the activity is terminating.

6. onRestart():

- Called when an activity in the Stopped state is about to restart, onRestart() restores the activity's state from the time it was stopped. This callback is always succeeded by onStart().

7. onDestroy():

- Executed before the activity is destroyed, onDestroy() is the final callback in the activity lifecycle. Typically used to release resources, it ensures that all activity-related resources are properly handled when the activity or the encompassing process is terminated.

Intents in Android

- An Intent serves as a messaging construct designed for communication between distinct Android components.
- It functions as a means to solicit a specific action from an app component.
- Intents play a pivotal role in fostering interaction between various Android components such as Activities, Services, and Content Providers.
- They act as conduits for instigating actions, allowing seamless communication among disparate components.
- The responsive nature of Android is facilitated by Intents, where the system listens for these messaging objects and reacts accordingly.
- The identification and invocation of the appropriate app component are determined by the content and purpose of the Intent.
- The versatility of Intents extends to communication within the same app as well as across different applications.
- This flexibility enables a robust and adaptable communication framework.
- In scenarios where multiple apps can respond to a particular Intent, Android presents users with a selection.
- This empowers users to choose the preferred app to carry out the intended action, providing a tailored and user-centric experience.

In summary, an Intent is a dynamic and versatile messaging mechanism, serving as a cornerstone for effective communication and action initiation across various Android components.

Uses of Intent in Android:

Intents in Android serve three fundamental purposes:

1. **To start an Activity:**
   - An Activity represents a distinct screen within an app.
   - Initiates a new instance of an Activity using `startActivity()` by passing an Intent.

- The Intent specifies the activity to start and carries any requisite data.

2. **To start a Service:**
   - A Service is a background component performing operations without a user interface.
   - Commences a service for one-time operations (e.g., file download) through `startService()` and an associated Intent.
   - The Intent delineates the service to start and includes any pertinent data.

3. **To deliver a Broadcast:**
   - Broadcasts are messages accessible to any app.
   - The system generates broadcasts for various system events like system boot-up or device charging.
   - Initiates a broadcast to other apps using `sendBroadcast()` or `sendOrderedBroadcast()` by passing an Intent.
   - The Intent specifies the type of broadcast and includes relevant data.

Types of Intents in Android:

1. **Explicit Intents:**
   - When you specifically say which part of your app should open in response to a user's action, you use explicit intents.
   - Example: Suppose you want to open a new screen or perform a background task like downloading a file; you use explicit intents because you know exactly which part of your app (activity or service) to start.

Creating an Explicit Intent:

i. Create an Intent object, specifying where you are (current activity) and where you want to go (target activity).

   Example: `Intent i = new Intent(this, TargetActivity.class);`

ii. Use startActivity() to go to the specified activity.

   Example: `startActivity(i);`

iii. If needed, use putExtra() to send information to the new activity.

   Example: `i.putExtra("key", "value");`

Note: *To access and utilize data sent to a new activity through an explicit intent, employ the* `getIntent()` *method in the Java class of the destination activity. Subsequently, use* `getStringExtra("key")` *to retrieve specific information based on the provided key during data transmission. The retrieved data, such as a string, can then be stored in a variable (e.g., String a) for subsequent use within the new activity. This process ensures seamless handling of transmitted data between different components in your Android app.*

```
String a = getIntent().getStringExtra("key1");
```

2. **Implicit Intent**

- Implicit intents simplify the process of declaring actions without specifying a particular component to perform them.
- Instead, they express a general action, allowing any compatible component, even from another app, to handle the intended action.
- For instance, if you aim to display a user's location on a map, an implicit intent can seamlessly pass the coordinates to any map-capable app.

Creating an Implicit Intent:

i. Instantiate an Intent object for implicit intents.

ii. Specify the desired action using action constants, defining the nature of the action.

```
Intent i = new Intent(Intent.ACTION_VIEW);
```

iii. The action, represented as a string, determines the structure of the intent and its data. Examples:
   a. ACTION_VIEW: Used to display information in an activity (e.g., a photo in a Gallery app or an address in a Map app).
   b. ACTION_SEND: Used to share data with other apps (e.g., Email or Social Networking apps).

iv. Supply data for the action using setData(), often expressed as a URI. Example:

```
i.setData(Uri.parse("http://www.google.co.in"));
```

v. Execute the action by calling startActivity() with the intent object as the parameter.

```
startActivity(i);
```

Working with Fragments

- A Fragment in Android serves as a self-contained and modular UI component that can be utilized within an activity.
- It operates independently, providing a distinct and reusable interface component that is associated with an activity.
- Although a fragment operates autonomously, its lifecycle is closely tied to that of the hosting activity.
- Consequently, when the associated activity is terminated or destroyed, the fragment undergoes a corresponding destruction.
- This interdependence allows fragments to contribute to the overall user interface of an activity while maintaining a level of independence and reusability.
- Fragments in Android boast their own set of lifecycle events distinct from those of activities, providing developers with fine-grained control over their behavior.
- While an activity can incorporate multiple fragments, it is advisable to exercise caution and avoid overwhelming a single activity with an excessive number of fragments.
- The reusability of fragments shines through, allowing a single fragment to be seamlessly integrated into multiple activities, enhancing code modularity.

Typically, fragments find their niche in constructing multi-pane user interfaces within Android applications. Each fragment possesses its own UI layout, but intriguingly, a fragment can be designed without any associated layout, functioning more like a background service without a visible user interface.

In essence, a fragment proves to be a versatile and powerful component in the Android OS, offering developers the flexibility to implement various functionalities and user interface designs in an app.

Fragment Lifecycle Overview:

The Fragment lifecycle unfolds with its attachment to an activity, progressing through various stages with corresponding methods:

i.   **onAttach(Activity):** Called once when the fragment is attached to the activity.

ii.   **onCreate(Bundle):** Invoked when the fragment is created, providing an essential space to initialize fragment components.

iii. **onCreateView():** Called when the fragment's UI is initialized, returning a View component. If the fragment lacks a UI, a null can be returned.

iv.   **onActivityCreated():** Triggered when the host activity is created, enabling access to the fragment's view using the findViewById() method.

v.   **onStart():** Executed when the fragment becomes visible on the device's screen.

vi.   **onResume():** Marks the fragment as resumed, signifying active interaction.

vii. **onPause():** Called when the fragment is no longer interactive and the user is about to leave. Ideal for saving session-related data.

viii. **onStop():** Executed when the fragment is no longer visible.

ix.   **onDestroyView():** Called when the fragment is about to be destroyed, allowing cleanup of resources before final destruction.

x.   **onDestroy():** Invoked for the fragment's final cleanup and state handling.

xi.   **onDetach():** Called just before the fragment is detached from the host activity.

Implementing Fragments

Indeed, understanding fragments sets the stage for practical implementation. To create a fragment, one must define a fragment class that extends the Fragment class and overrides essential methods. This allows for the customization and initialization of the fragment. By extending the Fragment class, developers gain access to a powerful set of methods that cater to various stages in the fragment lifecycle.

Here's a simplified example of creating a fragment class in Android:

```java
import android.os.Bundle;
import android.view.LayoutInflater;
import android.view.View;
import android.view.ViewGroup;

public class MyFragment extends Fragment {
    // Required empty public constructor
    public MyFragment() {
    }
    // Called when the fragment is created
    @Override
    public void onCreate(Bundle savedInstanceState) {
        super.onCreate(savedInstanceState);
        // Initialize fragment-specific components or data
    }
    // Called to create the fragment's UI
    @Override
    public View onCreateView(LayoutInflater inflater, ViewGroup container,
                             Bundle savedInstanceState) {
        // Inflate the layout for this fragment
        return inflater.inflate(R.layout.fragment_my, container, false);
    }
    // Other lifecycle methods can be overridden as needed
}
```

In this example, MyFragment extends the Fragment class, and key methods such as `onCreate()` and `onCreateView()` are overridden. The `onCreate()` method is where fragment-specific components or data can be initialized, while `onCreateView()` is responsible for inflating the fragment's UI layout.

CHAPTER 4

ANDROID COMPONENTS OVERVIEW

In the vast landscape of Android app development, a myriad of components forms the building blocks that collectively shape the user experience. These Android components, ranging from interactive buttons to dynamic RecyclerViews, are the elemental entities that developers orchestrate to craft seamless and engaging applications. Each component brings a unique functionality, be it handling user input, displaying content, or facilitating navigation. This comprehensive spectrum of Android components empowers developers to create versatile and feature-rich apps that cater to a diverse array of user interactions and preferences. In this exploration, we delve into the fundamental Android components that serve as the bedrock for constructing intuitive and visually appealing mobile applications.

In this chapter, we will navigate through the fundamental Android components, unraveling their functionalities and exploring how they synergize to shape the user interface and overall functionality of Android applications. From the basic building blocks like buttons and text views to more sophisticated elements such as Spinners and AlertDialog, our journey will provide a comprehensive understanding of the tools at an Android developer's disposal. With each section dedicated to a specific component, we aim to guide you through the intricacies of implementation, customization, and effective usage. Whether you are a novice venturing into Android app development or an experienced developer seeking to refine your skills, this chapter serves as a roadmap to harness the full potential of Android components in crafting exceptional user experiences.

Buttons in Android

- Buttons in Android are essential components that empower users to trigger actions within an application.
- They are interactive UI elements that respond to user clicks or touches, serving as a fundamental part of the user interface.
- Buttons are versatile components, allowing developers to initiate a wide range of actions, from simple alerts to complex navigations or data processing.
- Understanding the working of buttons is integral to creating intuitive and responsive Android applications.

Key Characteristics of Buttons:

1. **Click Event:** Buttons respond to user interactions through a click event. When a user taps or clicks on a button, a specific action is initiated.

2. **Text and Icons:** Buttons can include text labels and icons to convey their purpose. This makes the user interface more informative and user-friendly.

3. **States:** Buttons have different states such as normal, pressed, and disabled. These states help in providing visual feedback to users about the button's interactivity.

Working of a Button:

1. **XML Declaration:** In the XML layout file, you declare a Button element, specifying attributes like text, appearance, and layout parameters.

```
<Button
```

```
android:id="@+id/myButton"
android:layout_width="wrap_content"
android:layout_height="wrap_content"
android:text="Click Me" />
```

2. **Reference in Java Code:** In the corresponding Java code, you reference the button using its ID and define the click event.

```java
Button myButton = findViewById(R.id.myButton);
myButton.setOnClickListener(new View.OnClickListener() {
    @Override
    public void onClick(View view) {

        // Action to perform when the button is clicked
        // For example, show a message or navigate to another screen

    }
});
```

3. **Click Event Handling:** The setOnClickListener method is crucial for handling the click event. Inside the onClick method, you define the actions that should occur when the button is clicked.

```java
myButton.setOnClickListener(new View.OnClickListener() {
    @Override
    public void onClick(View view) {
        // Action to perform when the button is clicked
        // For example, show a message or navigate to another screen
        Toast.makeText(getApplicationContext(), "Button Clicked!",
Toast.LENGTH_SHORT).show();
    }
});
```

TextViews in Android

- TextViews in Android are fundamental components for displaying text within an application's user interface. Whether conveying information, presenting instructions, or showcasing dynamic content, TextViews play a crucial role in creating a coherent and informative user experience.
- TextViews provide a versatile canvas for displaying textual information, and their integration extends beyond mere static text.
- Let's delve into the workings of TextViews, exploring their attributes, customization options, and the essential steps to integrate them seamlessly into your Android application.

Key Characteristics of TextViews:

1. **Text Display:** TextViews are designed to display static and dynamic text content, providing a versatile means to communicate information to users.

2. **Formatting Options:** TextViews offer extensive formatting options, allowing developers to customize text appearance, including font size, color, style, and alignment.

3. **Support for Spannable Text:** TextViews support Spannable text, enabling the creation of text with different styles (e.g., bold, italic) or clickable links within the same TextView.

4. **Scrolling Capability:** For cases where the text content exceeds the available space, TextViews can be configured to support scrolling.

Working of a TextView:

1. **XML Declaration:** In the XML layout file, you declare a TextView element, specifying attributes like text, appearance, and layout parameters.

```xml
<TextView
    android:id="@+id/myTextView"
    android:layout_width="wrap_content"
    android:layout_height="wrap_content"
    android:text="Hello, TextView!"
    android:textSize="18sp"
    android:textColor="#333333"
    android:gravity="center" />
```

2. **Reference in Java Code:** In the corresponding Java code, you reference the TextView using its ID.

```java
TextView myTextView = findViewById(R.id.myTextView);
```

3. **Text Manipulation:** You can dynamically set or modify the text content of the TextView in your code.

```java
myTextView.setText("Updated Text");
```

4. **Text Appearance Customization:** TextViews offer methods to customize the appearance of text dynamically.

```java
myTextView.setTextSize(20); // Set text size
myTextView.setTextColor(Color.RED); // Set text color
```

ImageView in Android

- ImageViews in Android serve as the canvas for visual storytelling within an application.
- They play a pivotal role in presenting images, graphics, and visual elements to users, enhancing the overall aesthetic and communicative aspects of an app.
- Let's unravel the workings of ImageViews, exploring their attributes, customization options, and the essential steps to seamlessly integrate visual content into your Android application.

Key Characteristics of ImageViews:

1. **Image Display:** ImageViews are designed to display static or dynamically loaded images, offering a visual representation of content.

2. **Scale Types:** ImageViews support different scale types, allowing developers to control how images are resized and fitted within the view.

3. **Resource Loading:** Images can be loaded into ImageViews from various sources, including local resources, drawable files, or remotely from URLs.

4. **Customization:** Developers can customize the appearance of ImageViews, adjusting attributes such as image tint, rotation, and visibility.

Working of an ImageView:

1. **XML Declaration:** In the XML layout file, you declare an ImageView element, specifying attributes like the image source, appearance, and layout parameters.

```
<ImageView
    android:id="@+id/myImageView"
    android:layout_width="200dp"
    android:layout_height="200dp"
    android:src="@drawable/my_image"
    android:scaleType="centerCrop" />
```

2. **Reference in Java Code:** In the corresponding Java code, you reference the ImageView using its ID.

```
ImageView myImageView = findViewById(R.id.myImageView);
```

3. **Image Loading:** You can dynamically load images into the ImageView, either from local resources or external sources.

```
myImageView.setImageResource(R.drawable.new_image); // Load from resources
```

4. **Image Customization:** ImageViews offer methods to customize the appearance of loaded images dynamically.

```
myImageView.setRotation(90); // Rotate the image
myImageView.setColorFilter(Color.BLUE); // Apply a tint to the image
```

EditTexts in Android

- EditText in Android is a versatile UI element designed to capture and display text input from users.
- Whether soliciting usernames, passwords, or user-generated content, EditText provides a dynamic and interactive means for users to interact with your application.
- EditTexts are foundational for collecting user-generated content and facilitating various forms of user interaction.
- Whether used for simple text input or more complex scenarios, mastering the integration and customization of EditTexts is essential for creating dynamic and user-friendly Android applications.

- Let's explore the attributes, customization options, and the fundamental steps to seamlessly integrate EditText into your Android application.

Key Characteristics of EditText:

1. **Text Input:** EditText allows users to input and edit textual content, making it a fundamental component for forms, search bars, and text-based interactions.

2. **Keyboard Interaction:** When an EditText is selected, the keyboard automatically appears, allowing users to input text through a variety of input methods.

3. **Input Types:** EditText supports various input types, including text, numbers, passwords, and more, ensuring the appropriate keyboard layout is presented to users.

4. **Text Manipulation:** Developers can programmatically retrieve or modify the text within an EditText, enabling dynamic updates and validations.

Working of an EditText:

1. **XML Declaration:** In the XML layout file, you declare an EditText element, specifying attributes like input type, hint text, appearance, and layout parameters.

```xml
<EditText
    android:id="@+id/myEditText"
    android:layout_width="match_parent"
    android:layout_height="wrap_content"
    android:inputType="text"
    android:hint="Enter your text here" />
```

2. **Reference in Java Code:** In the corresponding Java code, you reference the EditText using its ID.

```java
EditText myEditText = findViewById(R.id.myEditText);
```

3. **Text Retrieval and Modification:** You can dynamically retrieve or modify the text content of the EditText in your code.

```java
String userInput = myEditText.getText().toString(); // Retrieve text

myEditText.setText("Updated Text"); // Set text programmatically
```

4. **Input Validation:** EditTexts can be used in conjunction with input validation logic to ensure that users provide the expected type of information.

```java
if (userInput.isEmpty()) {
    // Display an error message or take appropriate action
}
```

Spinners in Android

- A Spinner in Android is a user interface element that provides a dropdown menu of selectable items.
- It's a valuable component when you want users to choose from a list of options in a compact and visually appealing manner.
- Spinners are commonly used for selecting items such as categories, filters, or any other set of related choices.
- Spinners provide an elegant solution for presenting users with a set of choices in a way that conserves screen space.
- Whether used for selecting filters, preferences, or any other categorical options, mastering the integration and customization of Spinners is essential for crafting user-friendly and intuitive Android applications.
- Let's explore the attributes, customization options, and the fundamental steps to integrate Spinners seamlessly into your Android application.

Key Characteristics of Spinner:

1. **Dropdown Menu:** Spinner displays a dropdown menu containing a list of selectable items, making it a space-efficient choice for presenting a range of options.

2. **Adapter-Based:** Spinners are adapter-based, meaning they rely on an adapter to populate the list of items. This allows for dynamic and flexible data binding.

3. **Selection Feedback:** When a user selects an item from the Spinner, the selected item is visually displayed, providing immediate feedback on the chosen option.

4. **Event Handling:** Developers can implement event listeners to capture user interactions with the Spinner, enabling dynamic responses based on user selections.

Working of a Spinner:

1. **XML Declaration:** In the XML layout file, you declare a Spinner element, specifying attributes like item source, appearance, and layout parameters.

```xml
<Spinner
    android:id="@+id/mySpinner"
    android:layout_width="match_parent"
    android:layout_height="wrap_content"
    android:entries="@array/spinner_items" />
```

2. **Reference in Java Code:** In the corresponding Java code, you reference the Spinner using its ID.

```java
Spinner mySpinner = findViewById(R.id.mySpinner);
```

3. **Adapter Setup:** You need to set up an adapter to populate the Spinner with data. This can be done using an ArrayAdapter, for example.

```java
ArrayAdapter<CharSequence> adapter = ArrayAdapter.createFromResource(this,
R.array.spinner_items, android.R.layout.simple_spinner_item);
adapter.setDropDownViewResource(android.R.layout.simple_spinner_dropdown_item);
```

```
mySpinner.setAdapter(adapter);
```

4. **Item Selection Handling:** You can implement item selection handling to respond to user choices.

```
mySpinner.setOnItemSelectedListener(new
AdapterView.OnItemSelectedListener() {
    @Override
    public void onItemSelected(AdapterView<?> parentView, View
selectedItemView, int position, long id) {

        // Handle the selected item

    }

    @Override
    public void onNothingSelected(AdapterView<?> parentView) {

        // Handle case where nothing is selected

    }
});
```

CheckBoxes in Android

- Checkboxes in Android provide a simple yet effective way for users to make multiple selections or express binary choices.
- Whether it's confirming preferences, selecting items from a list, or enabling specific features, checkboxes enhance the interactive capabilities of your Android application.
- Checkboxes offer a straightforward way to incorporate user choices, preferences, and multiple selections into your Android app's interface.
- Whether used for enabling/disabling features or indicating user preferences, mastering the integration and customization of checkboxes is fundamental for creating interactive and user-friendly Android applications.
- Let's delve into the attributes, customization options, and the fundamental steps to seamlessly integrate Checkboxes into your Android user interface.

Key Characteristics of Checkboxes:

1. **Binary Selection:** Checkboxes represent a binary choice – users can either check (select) or uncheck (deselect) them.

2. **Multi-Selection:** Multiple checkboxes can be presented together, allowing users to make multiple selections from a list of options.

3. **User Feedback:** Checked and unchecked states provide visual feedback to users, conveying the current selection status.

4. **Event Handling:** Developers can implement event listeners to capture user interactions with checkboxes, facilitating dynamic responses based on user choices.

Working of a Checkbox:

1. **XML Declaration:** In the XML layout file, you declare a Checkbox element, specifying attributes like initial state, appearance, and layout parameters.

```xml
<CheckBox
    android:id="@+id/myCheckbox"
    android:layout_width="wrap_content"
    android:layout_height="wrap_content"
    android:text="Enable Feature" />
```

2. **Reference in Java Code:** In the corresponding Java code, you reference the Checkbox using its ID.

```java
CheckBox myCheckbox = findViewById(R.id.myCheckbox);
```

3. **Event Handling:** You can implement event handling to respond to user interactions with the Checkbox.

```java
myCheckbox.setOnCheckedChangeListener(new CompoundButton.OnCheckedChangeListener()
{
    @Override
    public void onCheckedChanged(CompoundButton buttonView, boolean isChecked) {

        // Respond to checkbox state change

        if (isChecked) {

            // Checkbox is checked

        } else {

            // Checkbox is unchecked

        }
    }
});
```

4. **Programmatic State Changes:** You can also programmatically set or query the state of a checkbox.

```java
myCheckbox.setChecked(true); // Set checkbox to checked state
```

RadioButtons in Android

- RadioButtons in Android are a user interface element that allows users to select a single option from a group of related choices.
- This exclusive selection mechanism makes RadioButtons suitable for scenarios where users need to choose only one option among several.
- Whether it's selecting a gender, choosing a payment method, or indicating a preference, RadioButtons provide an effective way to manage exclusive choices.

- RadioButtons provide a streamlined way to manage exclusive choices, ensuring that users can select only one option from a group.
- Whether used for survey questions, form inputs, or any scenario with mutually exclusive options, mastering the integration and customization of RadioButtons is essential for creating intuitive and user-friendly Android applications.
- Let's explore the attributes, customization options, and the fundamental steps to integrate RadioButtons seamlessly into your Android application.

Key Characteristics of RadioButtons:

1. **Exclusive Selection:** Users can select only one RadioButton from a group of related RadioButtons.

2. **Visual Indication:** The selected RadioButton is visually highlighted, providing immediate feedback to users.

3. **Grouping:** RadioButtons are often used in groups, known as RadioGroups, to enforce the exclusive selection behavior within the group.

4. **Event Handling:** Developers can implement event listeners to capture user interactions with RadioButtons and respond dynamically.

Working of RadioButtons:

1. **XML Declaration:** In the XML layout file, you declare a RadioButton element, specifying attributes like text, appearance, and layout parameters.

```
<RadioButton
    android:id="@+id/radioOption1"
    android:layout_width="wrap_content"
    android:layout_height="wrap_content"
    android:text="Option 1" />
```

2. **Grouping in XML:** If you want to enforce exclusive selection within a group, you can use a RadioGroup in the XML layout.

```
<RadioGroup
    android:id="@+id/radioGroupOptions"
    android:layout_width="wrap_content"
    android:layout_height="wrap_content">

    <RadioButton
        android:id="@+id/radioOption1"
        android:layout_width="wrap_content"
        android:layout_height="wrap_content"
        android:text="Option 1" />

    <RadioButton
        android:id="@+id/radioOption2"
```

```xml
        android:layout_width="wrap_content"
        android:layout_height="wrap_content"
        android:text="Option 2" />

    <!-- Add more RadioButtons as needed -->

</RadioGroup>
```

3. **Reference in Java Code:** In the corresponding Java code, you reference the RadioButton using its ID.

```java
RadioButton radioOption1 = findViewById(R.id.radioOption1);
```

4. **Event Handling:** You can implement event handling to respond to user interactions with RadioButtons.

```java
radioOption1.setOnCheckedChangeListener(new
CompoundButton.OnCheckedChangeListener() {
    @Override
    public void onCheckedChanged(CompoundButton buttonView, boolean
isChecked) {

        // Respond to RadioButton state change

        if (isChecked) {

            // RadioButton is selected

        } else {

            // RadioButton is deselected

        }
    }
});
```

ListView and RecyclerView

- Both ListView and RecyclerView are essential components in Android for displaying lists of data in a user-friendly and efficient manner.
- Whether you need to showcase contacts, messages, or any dynamic content, these components offer flexible solutions.
- ListView and RecyclerView cater to different needs, with RecyclerView offering more advanced features for complex list displays.
- While ListView remains suitable for simpler use cases, RecyclerView is preferred for its versatility and improved performance, especially when dealing with large datasets and varied layouts. Mastering the integration and customization of these components is crucial for creating dynamic and engaging Android applications.
- Let's explore the attributes, distinctions, and the fundamental steps to integrate ListView and RecyclerView seamlessly into your Android application.

Key Characteristics of ListView:

1. **Simple List Display:** ListView provides a straightforward way to display a vertical list of scrollable items.

2. **Adapter-Based:** Adapters are used to provide data to the ListView, enabling dynamic content based on the underlying data source.

3. **ArrayAdapter:** Commonly used ArrayAdapter simplifies the process of binding data to the ListView for simple use cases.

4. **Scrolling:** ListView efficiently handles scrolling through a potentially large dataset, recycling views as needed.

Working of ListView:

1. **XML Declaration:** In the XML layout file, you declare a ListView element.

```xml
<ListView
    android:id="@+id/myListView"
    android:layout_width="match_parent"
    android:layout_height="wrap_content" />
```

2. **Reference in Java Code:** In the corresponding Java code, you reference the ListView using its ID.

```java
ListView myListView = findViewById(R.id.myListView);
```

3. **Adapter Setup:** You need to set up an adapter to populate the ListView with data.

```java
ArrayAdapter<String> arrayAdapter = new ArrayAdapter<>(this,
android.R.layout.simple_list_item_1, myData);
myListView.setAdapter(arrayAdapter);
```

4. **Item Click Handling:** Implement event listeners to respond to user clicks on ListView items.

```java
myListView.setOnItemClickListener(new AdapterView.OnItemClickListener() {
    @Override
    public void onItemClick(AdapterView<?> parent, View view, int position,
long id) {

        // Respond to item click

    }
});
```


Key Characteristics of RecyclerView:

1. **Advanced List Display:** RecyclerView offers a more advanced and customizable way to display lists, surpassing the capabilities of ListView.

2. **Adapter and ViewHolder:** RecyclerView introduces the ViewHolder pattern for optimized view recycling, and a separate adapter is used to manage data binding.

3. **LayoutManager:** RecyclerView uses a LayoutManager to control the arrangement of items, providing flexibility for various layouts (linear, grid, etc.).

4. **Item Animations:** Supports built-in item animations for smooth user interactions.

Working of RecyclerView:

1. **XML Declaration:** In the XML layout file, you declare a RecyclerView element.

```
<androidx.recyclerview.widget.RecyclerView
    android:id="@+id/myRecyclerView"
    android:layout_width="match_parent"
    android:layout_height="wrap_content" />
```

2. **Reference in Java/Kotlin Code:** In the corresponding Java or Kotlin code, you reference the RecyclerView using its ID.

```
RecyclerView myRecyclerView = findViewById(R.id.myRecyclerView);
```

3. **Adapter Setup:** You need to set up a RecyclerView.Adapter to populate the RecyclerView with data.

```
MyRecyclerViewAdapter adapter = new MyRecyclerViewAdapter(myData);
myRecyclerView.setAdapter(adapter);
```

4. **LayoutManager Configuration:** Set up a LayoutManager to define how items should be arranged.

```
LinearLayoutManager layoutManager = new LinearLayoutManager(this);
myRecyclerView.setLayoutManager(layoutManager);
```

5. **Item Click Handling:** Implement item click handling if needed.

```
adapter.setOnItemClickListener(new
MyRecyclerViewAdapter.OnItemClickListener() {

    @Override

    public void onItemClick(int position) {

        // Respond to item click

    }

});
```

Seekbar in Android

- The SeekBar in Android is a user interface element that provides a visual representation of a range along with a draggable thumb.
- It allows users to select a specific value within a defined range by sliding the thumb along the SeekBar.
- This component is commonly used for scenarios where continuous or discrete adjustments are required, such as adjusting volume, brightness, or seeking through media playback.
- SeekBar in Android provides a visually intuitive way for users to interactively adjust values within a specified range.
- Whether used for adjusting settings, controlling media playback, or any scenario that requires continuous or discrete adjustments, SeekBar offers a versatile solution.
- Mastering the integration and customization of SeekBar is crucial for enhancing the user experience in Android applications that require interactive control elements.

Key Characteristics of SeekBar:

1. **Visual Representation:** The SeekBar visually represents a range with a draggable thumb that users can slide to select a specific value.

2. **Numeric Range:** SeekBar is often associated with a numeric range, allowing users to select a value within that range.

3. **Continuous or Discrete:** Depending on the use case, SeekBar can be configured for continuous values (e.g., volume adjustment) or discrete steps (e.g., selecting from a predefined list).

4. **Event Handling:** Developers can implement event listeners to capture changes in the SeekBar's value and respond dynamically.

Working of SeekBar:

1. **XML Declaration:** In the XML layout file, you declare a SeekBar element.

```
<SeekBar
    android:id="@+id/mySeekBar"
    android:layout_width="match_parent"
    android:layout_height="wrap_content" />
```

2. **Reference in Java Code:** In the corresponding Java or Kotlin code, you reference the SeekBar using its ID.

```
SeekBar mySeekBar = findViewById(R.id.mySeekBar);
```

3. **Event Handling:** You can implement event handling to respond to changes in the SeekBar's value.

```
mySeekBar.setOnSeekBarChangeListener(new SeekBar.OnSeekBarChangeListener()
{
    @Override
    public void onProgressChanged(SeekBar seekBar, int progress, boolean fromUser) {
```

```java
        // Respond to progress change
    }

    @Override
    public void onStartTrackingTouch(SeekBar seekBar) {
        // Called when user starts dragging the thumb
    }

    @Override
    public void onStopTrackingTouch(SeekBar seekBar) {
        // Called when user stops dragging the thumb
    }
});
```

4. **Customization:** SeekBar can be customized further by adjusting attributes such as range, appearance, and orientation (horizontal or vertical).

```java
// Set maximum value of the SeekBar
mySeekBar.setMax(100);

// Set initial progress
mySeekBar.setProgress(50);
```

5. **Numeric Display:** Optionally, you can display the current progress numerically.

```java
// Display the current progress numerically
int currentProgress = mySeekBar.getProgress();
```

ProgressBar in Android

- The ProgressBar in Android is a graphical user interface element used to visualize the progress of a task or operation.
- It provides visual feedback to users, indicating that a process is ongoing and conveying an estimate of how much of the task has been completed.
- ProgressBars are commonly used in scenarios such as file downloads, data uploads, and any operation where the duration or completion status is uncertain.
- ProgressBar in Android serves as a crucial visual element for keeping users informed about ongoing tasks.
- Whether in determinate mode, providing a clear indication of progress, or in indeterminate mode, signaling ongoing activity, ProgressBar enhances the user experience by reducing uncertainty. The effective integration and customization of ProgressBar are essential skills for developers aiming to create polished Android applications with dynamic and responsive user interfaces.

Key Characteristics of ProgressBar:

1. **Visual Feedback:** ProgressBar visually communicates the progress of a task through a visual indicator that fills or moves across the ProgressBar.

2. **Determinate and Indeterminate Modes:** It can operate in determinate mode, where the progress is measurable and known, or indeterminate mode, where the duration or completion status is uncertain.

3. **Customization:** Developers can customize the appearance of the ProgressBar, adjusting attributes such as color, style, and size.

4. **Event Handling:** ProgressBars can be associated with event listeners to execute specific actions when the progress changes or when the task is completed.

Working of ProgressBar:

1. **XML Declaration:** In the XML layout file, you declare a ProgressBar element.

```xml
<ProgressBar
    android:id="@+id/myProgressBar"
    android:layout_width="match_parent"
    android:layout_height="wrap_content"
    style="?android:attr/progressBarStyleHorizontal" />
```

2. **Reference in Java/Kotlin Code:** In the corresponding Java or Kotlin code, you reference the ProgressBar using its ID.

```java
ProgressBar myProgressBar = findViewById(R.id.myProgressBar);
```

3. **Setting Progress:** You can set the progress of the ProgressBar based on the completion of the task.

```java
// Set determinate progress
myProgressBar.setProgress(50);

// Set indeterminate mode
myProgressBar.setIndeterminate(true);
```

4. **Event Handling:** Implement event listeners to respond to changes in the ProgressBar's progress.

```java
myProgressBar.setOnSeekBarChangeListener(new
SeekBar.OnSeekBarChangeListener() {
    @Override
    public void onProgressChanged(SeekBar seekBar, int progress, boolean
fromUser) {

        // Respond to progress change

    }

    @Override
    public void onStartTrackingTouch(SeekBar seekBar) {

        // Called when user starts dragging the thumb
```

```
    }

    @Override
    public void onStopTrackingTouch(SeekBar seekBar) {

        // Called when user stops dragging the thumb

    }
});
```

5. **Customization:** Customize the appearance of the ProgressBar based on the application's design.

```
// Change the color of the ProgressBar
myProgressBar.getIndeterminateDrawable().setColorFilter(
    Color.BLUE, android.graphics.PorterDuff.Mode.SRC_IN);
```

TabLayout and ViewPager

- TabLayout and ViewPager are essential components in Android used to create an organized and navigable user interface, particularly for applications with multiple screens or content sections.
- TabLayout provides a set of horizontal tabs, and ViewPager allows users to swipe between different fragments or pages associated with each tab.
- TabLayout and ViewPager in Android provide an effective means of organizing and navigating content, enhancing the overall user experience. The combination of tabs for navigation and swipe gestures for content switching makes these components particularly valuable for applications with diverse content sections.

Key Characteristics of TabLayout and ViewPager:

- **TabLayout:**
    1. **Tab Navigation:** TabLayout facilitates the creation of a set of tabs, typically displayed horizontally, allowing users to navigate between different sections or categories.
    2. **Customization:** Developers can customize the appearance of tabs, including text color, indicator color, and other styling attributes.
    3. **Interactive:** Tabs are interactive, and users can tap on them to switch between associated content.
- **ViewPager:**
    1. **Swipe Navigation:** ViewPager enables the implementation of swipe gestures to navigate between fragments or pages associated with each tab.
    2. **Dynamic Content:** ViewPager is often paired with fragments, allowing dynamic loading and updating of content for each tab.
    3. **Efficient Memory Usage:** ViewPager is memory-efficient as it loads and retains a limited number of pages around the current page, optimizing performance.

Working of TabLayout and ViewPager:

1. **XML Declaration:** In the XML layout file, you declare a TabLayout and a ViewPager.

```
<com.google.android.material.tabs.TabLayout
```

```
    android:id="@+id/myTabLayout"
    android:layout_width="match_parent"
    android:layout_height="wrap_content"
    app:tabMode="fixed"
    app:tabGravity="fill" />

<androidx.viewpager.widget.ViewPager
    android:id="@+id/myViewPager"
    android:layout_width="match_parent"
    android:layout_height="match_parent" />
```

2. **Reference in Java Code:** Reference the TabLayout and ViewPager in your Java code.

```
TabLayout myTabLayout = findViewById(R.id.myTabLayout);
ViewPager myViewPager = findViewById(R.id.myViewPager);
```

3. **Adapter Setup:** Set up a ViewPager adapter to associate fragments with each tab.

```
MyPagerAdapter pagerAdapter = new MyPagerAdapter(getSupportFragmentManager());
myViewPager.setAdapter(pagerAdapter);

// Link the TabLayout and ViewPager
myTabLayout.setupWithViewPager(myViewPager);
```

4. **Fragment Implementation:** Implement fragments for each tab, providing the content or functionality associated with that tab.

```
public class MyFragment extends Fragment {

    // Fragment implementation

}
```

5. **Customization:** Customize the appearance of tabs and ViewPager based on design requirements.

```
// Customize TabLayout appearance
myTabLayout.setTabTextColors(Color.WHITE, Color.BLUE);

// Customize ViewPager appearance
myViewPager.setPageTransformer(true, new ZoomOutPageTransformer());
```

6. **Event Handling:** Implement event handling for interactions with tabs or ViewPager.

```
myTabLayout.addOnTabSelectedListener(new TabLayout.OnTabSelectedListener() {
    @Override
    public void onTabSelected(TabLayout.Tab tab) {

        // Handle tab selection
```

```java
    }

    @Override
    public void onTabUnselected(TabLayout.Tab tab) {

        // Handle tab unselection

    }

    @Override
    public void onTabReselected(TabLayout.Tab tab) {

        // Handle tab reselection

    }
});
```

Toast in Android

- In Android, a Toast is a simple and non-intrusive way to display brief messages or notifications to users.
- Toasts provide a quick and temporary visual cue, typically appearing at the bottom of the screen, to convey information or feedback about an operation.
- Toasts are valuable for delivering lightweight notifications without disrupting the user experience.
- Developers should use them judiciously for providing quick feedback or information in situations where a brief, unobtrusive message is appropriate.
- While Toasts are not suitable for conveying critical information or complex interactions, they are effective for enhancing the overall user experience in Android applications.

Key Characteristics of Toast:

1. **Brief Messages:** Toasts are designed for short, non-intrusive messages that quickly inform users about the status or result of an action.
2. **Temporary Display:** Toasts automatically disappear after a short duration, ensuring they don't linger on the screen and interrupt the user experience.
3. **Minimalistic Design:** They are usually displayed as small, unobtrusive pop-ups at the bottom of the screen, avoiding interference with the main content.

Working of Toast:

1. **Creating a Toast:** To create a Toast, use the Toast.makeText() method, providing the application's context, the message to be displayed, and the duration for which the Toast should be visible.

```java
Toast.makeText(context, "This is a Toast message", Toast.LENGTH_SHORT).show();
```

2. **Setting Duration:** The duration parameter specifies how long the Toast message should be visible. Use Toast.LENGTH_SHORT for a brief display or Toast.LENGTH_LONG for a slightly longer duration.

```
Toast.makeText(context, "Short Toast", Toast.LENGTH_SHORT).show();

Toast.makeText(context, "Long Toast", Toast.LENGTH_LONG).show();
```

3. **Displaying the Toast:** Call the show() method on the Toast object to display it.

```
toast.show();
```

4. **Customizing Appearance:** While Toasts have a default appearance, developers can customize them by changing the layout or using a custom view.

```
Toast customToast = new Toast(context);
customToast.setView(customView);
customToast.show();
```

5. **Positioning the Toast:** By default, Toasts appear at the bottom of the screen. To change the position, use the setGravity() method.

```
toast.setGravity(Gravity.TOP | Gravity.START, 0, 0);
```

6. **Handling Interaction:** Toasts are primarily for displaying information and don't support user interaction. For interactive elements, consider using dialogs or other UI components.

7. **Incorporating in Code:** Toasts are commonly used to provide feedback after a user action, such as clicking a button or completing a task.

```
Button myButton = findViewById(R.id.myButton);

myButton.setOnClickListener(v -> {

    Toast.makeText(context, "Button Clicked!", Toast.LENGTH_SHORT).show();

});
```

8. **Context Consideration:** Ensure that the context used to create the Toast is valid and associated with the current state of the application.

```
Toast.makeText(getApplicationContext(), "Context-aware Toast",
Toast.LENGTH_SHORT).show();
```

AlertDialog

- An AlertDialog in Android is a versatile component used to display alert messages, notifications, or interactive dialogs to users.
- It is a crucial element for conveying important information, confirming actions, or capturing user input within a popup dialog box.

- The AlertDialog component is a crucial tool for enhancing user interaction and communication in Android applications. By following the working principles outlined above, developers can create informative, interactive, and customizable dialog boxes tailored to their app's requirements.
- AlertDialogs are particularly valuable for handling user decisions, providing feedback, and ensuring a smooth and user-friendly experience.

Key Characteristics of AlertDialog:

1. **Popup Dialog:** AlertDialog appears as a popup dialog box, typically overlaid on the current activity, providing a focused interaction.

2. **Informative Messages:** It is commonly used to display informative messages, warnings, or alerts to users.

3. **Buttons and Actions:** AlertDialogs can include buttons for actions such as OK, Cancel, or custom actions, making them interactive.

4. **Customizable Appearance:** Developers can customize the appearance, layout, and behavior of AlertDialogs to suit the app's design.

Working of AlertDialog:

1. **Creating AlertDialog:** Instantiate an AlertDialog.Builder object, which is used to configure and build the AlertDialog.

```
AlertDialog.Builder builder = new AlertDialog.Builder(context);
```

2. **Setting Title and Message:** Set the title and message to be displayed in the AlertDialog.

```
builder.setTitle("Alert Title")
       .setMessage("This is an important message.");
```

3. **Adding Buttons:** Add buttons to the AlertDialog, specifying the text and actions for each button.

```
builder.setPositiveButton("OK", (dialog, which) -> {

    // Action to perform when OK button is clicked

});

builder.setNegativeButton("Cancel", (dialog, which) -> {

    // Action to perform when Cancel button is clicked

});
```

4. **Creating and Showing AlertDialog:** Create the AlertDialog by calling the create() method on the builder, and then show it.

```
AlertDialog alertDialog = builder.create();
alertDialog.show();
```

5. **Handling Button Clicks:** Implement any necessary logic or actions based on the user's button clicks.

```java
alertDialog.getButton(DialogInterface.BUTTON_POSITIVE).setOnClickListener(v -> {

    // Custom action for positive button click

});
```

6. **Customizing Appearance:** Customize the appearance and behavior of the AlertDialog, such as setting a custom layout.

```java
LayoutInflater inflater = getLayoutInflater();
View customLayout = inflater.inflate(R.layout.custom_alert_layout, null);
builder.setView(customLayout);
```

7. **Receiving User Input:** If needed, include input elements in the AlertDialog to capture user input.

```java
builder.setView(inputEditText);
```

8. **Displaying Single Choice Items:** Show a list of single-choice items within the AlertDialog.

```java
CharSequence[] items = {"Option 1", "Option 2", "Option 3"};

builder.setSingleChoiceItems(items, checkedItem, (dialog, which) -> {
    // Action to perform when a single item is selected
});
```

9. **Multi-Choice Items:** Allow users to select multiple items from a list.

```java
boolean[] checkedItems = {true, false, true};
builder.setMultiChoiceItems(items, checkedItems, (dialog, which, isChecked) -> {

    // Action to perform when a multi-choice item is selected or deselected

});
```

CHAPTER 5

ADVANCE ANDROID

Advancing in Android development involves mastering more sophisticated concepts and adopting practices that enhance the efficiency and scalability of your applications.

Architectural patterns play a crucial role in organizing code. As you progress, understanding patterns like MVVM (Model-View-ViewModel) becomes essential. MVVM separates concerns, making it easier to manage app logic and improve code maintainability.

Dependency injection is another critical concept. It simplifies the management of dependencies and enhances code modularity. Frameworks like Dagger 2 are widely used to implement dependency injection effectively.

Reactive programming is a paradigm shift that simplifies handling app events and data streams. RxJava is a popular framework that provides a toolbox for reactive programming, making asynchronous tasks and data handling more streamlined.

Modern UI development with Jetpack Compose is a significant step forward. Compose is a modern Android UI toolkit that simplifies UI development with a more declarative and concise syntax, offering a fresh way to create engaging user interfaces.

Mastering the creation of custom UI elements is an advanced skill. Understanding how to build unique and visually appealing components enhances the overall user experience, allowing developers to create more personalized interfaces.

Advanced networking skills are crucial for handling secure API calls, managing authentication, and optimizing network requests. This involves implementing secure communication practices to ensure data privacy and app security.

Testing techniques evolve as developers advance in their Android journey. This includes embracing various testing methodologies such as unit testing, integration testing, and UI testing to ensure robust and bug-free applications.

Performance optimization becomes a key consideration. Profiling tools help identify performance bottlenecks, and optimization strategies are employed to ensure smooth and efficient app execution.

Understanding security best practices is paramount. As applications become more sophisticated, safeguarding user data, implementing encryption, and ensuring secure communication become integral parts of development.

Mastery of Material Design principles is essential for creating visually appealing and user-friendly interfaces. Staying updated on the latest design trends ensures that applications adhere to contemporary design standards.

Publishing apps on Google Play requires a nuanced understanding of app signing, release management, and effective strategies to enhance app visibility and user engagement.

In conclusion, advancing in Android development involves a holistic approach, combining architectural understanding, coding practices, UI design mastery, and a keen focus on security and performance. Continuous learning and engagement with the Android community are crucial for staying at the forefront of this dynamic field.

MVVM Architecture

MVVM (Model-View-ViewModel) is an architectural pattern widely adopted in Android development for creating well-organized and maintainable applications. MVVM, which stands for Model-View-ViewModel, is an architectural pattern used in software development, particularly in building user interfaces. MVVM is designed to address the challenges of organizing and maintaining code in applications, offering a structured approach that separates concerns and enhances testability. It separates the concerns of an application into three main components: Model, View, and ViewModel.

1. **Model:**

    - The Model represents the data and business logic of the application.
    - It is responsible for managing and manipulating data, interacting with databases, APIs, or any other data sources.
    - The Model notifies the ViewModel about changes in the data.

2. **View:**

    - The View is responsible for displaying the user interface and capturing user input.
    - In Android, the View typically consists of Activities, Fragments, and XML layout files.
    - The View observes changes in the ViewModel and updates the UI accordingly.

3. **ViewModel:**

    - The ViewModel acts as an intermediary between the Model and the View.
    - It contains the application's business logic, processes data from the Model, and prepares it for the View.
    - It is not bound to the Android framework, making it easier to test.
    - The ViewModel exposes observable data streams that the View can observe. This is usually done using LiveData or RxJava.

Key Characteristics of MVVM in Android:

- **Data Binding:** MVVM is often used in conjunction with Android Data Binding. Data Binding allows you to bind UI components in the layout directly to the ViewModel, reducing boilerplate code and simplifying the interaction between the View and ViewModel.

- **Lifecycle Awareness:** ViewModel is designed to be lifecycle-aware, meaning it can be scoped to the lifecycle of an Activity or Fragment. This ensures that the ViewModel is only retained as long as the associated UI component is alive, preventing memory leaks.

- **Testability:** MVVM promotes testability by separating concerns. Since business logic is encapsulated in the ViewModel, it can be easily unit-tested without requiring the Android framework.

- **Reduced Fragmentation:** MVVM helps mitigate issues related to configuration changes (like screen rotations) by retaining the ViewModel during these changes. This ensures that the data is not lost, providing a smoother user experience.

Workflow of MVVM:

The MVVM (Model-View-ViewModel) architecture in Android follows a clear workflow that separates the concerns of the application into three main components. Let's delve into the detailed workflow of MVVM:

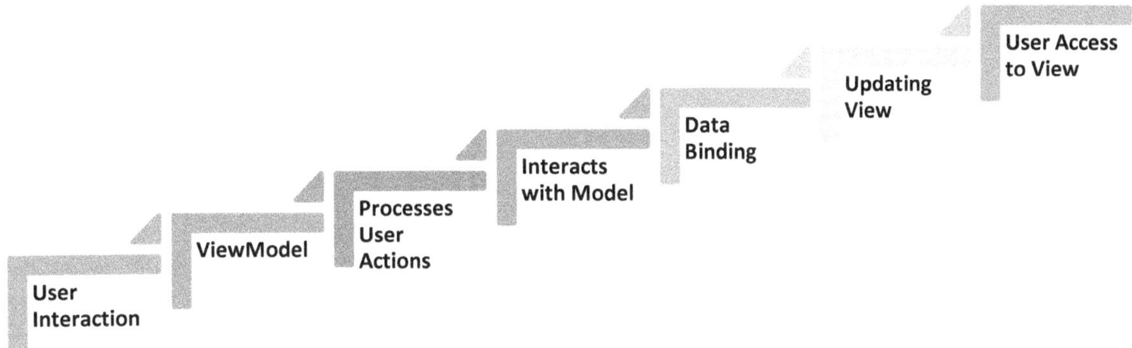

1. **User Interaction (View):**

   - The workflow begins with user interaction with the application's UI, which is represented by the View. This could be activities, fragments, or other UI components.
   - Views capture user input, such as button clicks, text input, or gestures.

2. **View Notification to ViewModel:**

   - The View notifies the associated ViewModel about user actions or events. This notification is typically done through data binding, observers, or other communication mechanisms.
   - The ViewModel is not directly aware of the View; instead, it exposes observable properties and methods that the View observes.

3. **ViewModel Processes User Actions:**

   - Upon receiving the notification, the ViewModel processes the user's action. It may involve business logic, data manipulation, or interaction with the Model layer.
   - The ViewModel prepares data for presentation, transforming and formatting it as needed.

4. **ViewModel Interacts with Model:**

   - The ViewModel interacts with the Model to fetch or update data. The Model represents the application's data layer, which may include databases, APIs, or other data sources.
   - The ViewModel is responsible for coordinating these interactions and handling the results.

5. **Data Binding (Optional):**
   - If data binding is used, the ViewModel updates the observable properties, and these changes are automatically reflected in the associated View. This simplifies the code by eliminating the need for explicit UI updates.

6. **ViewModel Updates View:**

- The ViewModel updates the View with the processed data or any changes that need to be reflected in the UI. This update is done using the observed properties or other communication mechanisms.
- The View is updated without having direct knowledge of the business logic or data fetching processes.

7. **User Sees Updated View:**

- The updated View is displayed to the user, showing the results of their actions or any changes in the application's state.
- The user can continue interacting with the UI, and the cycle repeats as needed.

Android Multimedia

Android devices offer a rich multimedia experience, supporting various types of media content such as audio, video, and images. Developers can leverage the Android Multimedia Framework to create engaging and feature-rich multimedia applications. Here's an overview of key components and functionalities:

1. **MediaPlayer Class:** The MediaPlayer class in Android is a versatile component for playing audio and video files. It supports various audio and video formats, providing methods for playback control, volume adjustment, and more.

Example of playing audio:

```
MediaPlayer mediaPlayer = MediaPlayer.create(context, R.raw.audio_file);
mediaPlayer.start();  // Start playback
```

Remember to release the MediaPlayer when done to free up resources:

```
mediaPlayer.release();
```

2. **MediaRecorder Class:** The MediaRecorder class is used for recording audio and video. It provides methods to set up the recording parameters, start and stop the recording process.

Example of recording audio:

```
MediaRecorder mediaRecorder = new MediaRecorder();
mediaRecorder.setAudioSource(MediaRecorder.AudioSource.MIC);
mediaRecorder.setOutputFormat(MediaRecorder.OutputFormat.THREE_GPP);
mediaRecorder.setOutputFile("output.3gp");
mediaRecorder.setAudioEncoder(MediaRecorder.AudioEncoder.AMR_NB);
mediaRecorder.prepare();
mediaRecorder.start();  // Start recording
```

Remember to stop and release the MediaRecorder when the recording is complete:

```
mediaRecorder.stop();
mediaRecorder.release();
```

3. **SurfaceView for Video Playback:** For video playback, developers often use SurfaceView in conjunction with MediaPlayer to display videos. SurfaceView provides a dedicated drawing surface, making it suitable for handling video frames efficiently.

4. **ExoPlayer:** The ExoPlayer library is a powerful alternative to the standard MediaPlayer for media playback. It supports advanced features like adaptive streaming, dynamic buffering, and a modular architecture. To use ExoPlayer, you need to include its dependencies in your project.

5. **ImageView for Image Display:** For displaying images, the ImageView widget is commonly used. Developers can load images from various sources, such as resources, URLs, or the device's storage, into an ImageView.

```
ImageView imageView = findViewById(R.id.imageView);
imageView.setImageResource(R.drawable.image_file);
```

6. **Glide Library:** Glide is a popular image loading library for Android that simplifies the process of loading and caching images. It provides features like image resizing, placeholder, and error handling.

```
// Using Glide to load an image from a URL
Glide.with(context).load("https://example.com/image.jpg").into(imageView);
```

7. **Android Camera API:** Android provides a Camera API for capturing photos and videos using the device's camera. The Camera API has been deprecated in recent Android versions, and developers are encouraged to use CameraX or third-party libraries for camera-related functionalities.

```
// Example code for opening the camera
Intent intent = new Intent(MediaStore.ACTION_IMAGE_CAPTURE);
startActivityForResult(intent, CAMERA_REQUEST_CODE);
```

These are fundamental components and tools for handling multimedia in Android applications. Depending on your specific requirements, you may explore additional libraries and APIs for more advanced multimedia features. Always consider handling media operations asynchronously to ensure a smooth user experience.

Shared Preferences

Android provides a convenient way to store and retrieve small amounts of data using Shared Preferences. This storage option allows developers to save and retrieve primitive data types, such as strings, integers, floats, and booleans, as key/value pairs in an XML file on the device's storage. Think of Shared Preferences as a dictionary where you associate keys with corresponding values. For instance, you could have a key "username" associated with the user's username.

How Shared Preferences Work

Shared Preferences are useful for scenarios where user settings or data need to persist across sessions, even if the app is killed, restarted, or the device is rebooted. Unlike an activity's instance state, data stored using Shared

Preferences is private within the application scope. It's commonly used to store user preferences, making it accessible across different activities within the app.

Shared Preferences vs. Saved Instance State

- Shared Preferences persist data across user sessions, even through app restarts or device reboots, making them ideal for storing user preferences or game scores. In contrast, Saved Instance State preserves state data across instances within the same user session, typically used for recreating the state after a device rotation.
- Shared Preferences persist data across sessions, making them suitable for long-term storage. Saved Instance State is focused on preserving data within the current session.
- Shared Preferences are suitable for storing user preferences, settings, or data that should be remembered across app launches. Saved Instance State is used to handle temporary changes in the activity's state.
- Shared Preferences store data as key/value pairs in an XML file. Saved Instance State stores data in a Bundle within the activity's instance state.
- Shared Preferences are not impacted by the activity's lifecycle changes. Saved Instance State is closely tied to the activity's lifecycle and is used for handling temporary state changes.
- Shared Preferences are best suited for persisting data that needs to survive beyond the current session, while Saved Instance State is used for maintaining state information within the same session, especially during configuration changes. Choosing between them depends on the specific requirements of the data and the desired persistence behavior.

Creating Shared Preferences

To create Shared Preferences, a unique file per app is generated using the package name. The `getSharedPreferences()` method is used, providing the file name and context mode (MODE_PRIVATE for secure private files). Shared Preferences can be edited using `SharedPreferences.Editor`. Modes like `MODE_PUBLIC, MODE_PRIVATE`, and `MODE_APPEND` cater to different access levels and file manipulation scenarios.

Methods of Shared Preferences

Shared Preferences provide various methods, including:

- **contains(String key):** Checks if a preference contains a certain key.
- **edit():** Creates a new editor for modifying data in preferences.
- **getAll():** Retrieves all values from preferences.
- **getBoolean(String key, boolean defValue):** Retrieves a boolean value.
- **getFloat(String key, float defValue):** Retrieves a float value.
- **getInt(String key, int defValue):** Retrieves an int value.
- **getLong(String key, long defValue):** Retrieves a long value.
- **getString(String key, String defValue):** Retrieves a String value.
- **getStringSet(String key, Set defValues):** Retrieves a set of String values.
- **registerOnSharedPreferenceChangeListener(SharedPreferences.OnSharedPreferenceChangeListener listener):** Registers a callback for preference changes.
- **unregisterOnSharedPreferenceChangeListener(SharedPreferences.OnSharedPreferenceChangeListener listener):** Unregisters a callback.

Sample Code for Storing and Retrieving Data in Shared Preferences

Here's a brief code snippet demonstrating how to store and retrieve data using Shared Preferences:

```
// Storing data into SharedPreferences
SharedPreferences sharedPreferences = getSharedPreferences("MySharedPref",
MODE_PRIVATE);
SharedPreferences.Editor myEdit = sharedPreferences.edit();
myEdit.putString("name", name.getText().toString());
myEdit.putInt("age", Integer.parseInt(age.getText().toString()));
myEdit.apply();

// Retrieving data from SharedPreferences

SharedPreferences sh = getSharedPreferences("MySharedPref", MODE_PRIVATE);
String s1 = sh.getString("name", "");
int a = sh.getInt("age", 0);
```

The provided example demonstrates a simple app with two EditTexts that save and retain user-entered data using Shared Preferences. This functionality is common in applications with forms, ensuring users don't have to re-enter details. The MainActivity file handles storing and retrieving data during the app's lifecycle.

Internal Storage

Internal storage is the dedicated space within the device's internal memory, reserved for an app's private use. This storage is secure, as it is exclusive to the app, and data stored here is inaccessible to other apps. It is ideal for storing sensitive user information and app-specific configuration files.

For file operations in internal storage, Android provides APIs through the Context class. The openFileOutput() and openFileInput() methods facilitate writing and reading files, while getFilesDir() obtains the path to the app's internal storage directory.

```
// Writing to internal storage
FileOutputStream fos = context.openFileOutput("filename.txt",
Context.MODE_PRIVATE);
fos.write(data.getBytes());
fos.close();

// Reading from internal storage
FileInputStream fis = context.openFileInput("filename.txt");
BufferedReader br = new BufferedReader(new InputStreamReader(fis));
String line = br.readLine();
```

External Storage

External storage refers to shared storage accessible by multiple apps and users. It includes external SD cards and other shared locations. Data stored here is public and can be accessed by other apps with the necessary permissions. External storage is suitable for storing media files and large downloads intended for sharing.

Standard Java I/O classes, such as FileInputStream and FileOutputStream, are used for file operations in external storage. The root directory of external storage can be obtained using `Environment.getExternalStorageDirectory()`.

```java
// Writing to external storage
File file = new File(Environment.getExternalStorageDirectory(),
"filename.txt");
FileOutputStream fos = new FileOutputStream(file);
fos.write(data.getBytes());
fos.close();

// Reading from external storage
FileInputStream fis = new FileInputStream(file);
BufferedReader br = new BufferedReader(new InputStreamReader(fis));
String line = br.readLine();
```

APIs in Android

API, which stands for Application Programming Interface, is a set of rules and tools that allows different software applications to communicate with each other. In the context of Android development, APIs play a crucial role in enabling communication between different components of an application, as well as facilitating interactions with external services, libraries, or platforms. Let's explore the key aspects of APIs in Android:

- **Android API:**
    - The Android API is a collection of libraries and packages provided by the Android operating system to facilitate the development of Android applications.
    - It includes classes and methods that developers can use to access device features, such as camera, sensors, network connectivity, and more.
    - Android API levels represent different versions of the Android platform, and developers can target specific API levels to ensure compatibility with different devices.

- **Web APIs:**
    - Web APIs (also known as RESTful APIs) enable communication between an Android app and a server or external service over the internet.
    - They use standard HTTP methods (GET, POST, PUT, DELETE) for operations and typically exchange data in a format like JSON or XML.
    - Developers use HTTP requests to interact with these APIs, sending requests to retrieve data, submit data, or perform other actions.

- **Third-Party APIs:**
    - Android developers often integrate third-party APIs into their applications to leverage external services or functionalities.
    - Examples include social media APIs (e.g., Facebook, Twitter), payment APIs (e.g., PayPal), mapping APIs (e.g., Google Maps), and more.
    - Developers need to obtain API keys or authentication tokens to securely access and use these services.

- **API Integration:**

- To integrate an API into an Android app, developers typically use libraries like Retrofit or Volley for making HTTP requests and handling responses.
  - Authentication mechanisms such as API keys, OAuth, or tokens are employed to secure communication between the app and the API.

- **Documentation:**
  - API documentation provides detailed information about the available endpoints, request and response formats, authentication requirements, and usage guidelines.
  - It serves as a guide for developers on how to interact with the API effectively.

- **Asynchronous Communication:**
  - API calls are often made asynchronously to avoid blocking the main thread of the application and provide a smoother user experience.
  - Callbacks, listeners, or reactive programming paradigms are used to handle asynchronous responses.

In summary, APIs in Android enable developers to access device functionalities, communicate with servers and external services, and enhance the functionality of their applications by integrating third-party services. Proper understanding of API usage and integration is essential for building robust and feature-rich Android applications.

JSON Parsing

JSON (JavaScript Object Notation) is a widely used data interchange format for communication between a server and a client or different components within an application. Android developers often encounter JSON when working with APIs to retrieve or send data. The following guide provides insights into JSON parsing in Android, focusing on the Gson library for its simplicity and efficiency.

In Android, JSON parsing can be achieved using the built-in org.json package, but for a more developer-friendly approach, third-party libraries like Gson are preferred. To incorporate Gson into your project, add the following dependency in your build.gradle file:

```
implementation 'com.google.code.gson:gson:2.8.9'
```

Next, create a Java class that mirrors the structure of your JSON data. Each field in the class should correspond to a key in the JSON object. For instance:

```java
public class Person {
    private String name;
    private int age;
    private String city;
    private boolean isStudent;
    private List<Integer> grades;

    // Getters and setters
}
```

Now, you can parse a JSON string into a Java object using Gson:

```java
String jsonString = "{ \"name\": \"John Doe\", \"age\": 25, \"city\": \"New York\", \"isStudent\": false, \"grades\": [85, 90, 78] }";
```

```java
Gson gson = new Gson();
Person person = gson.fromJson(jsonString, Person.class);
```

Once parsed, you can access the data using the Java object:

```java
String name = person.getName();
int age = person.getAge();
String city = person.getCity();
boolean isStudent = person.isStudent();
List<Integer> grades = person.getGrades();
```

Handling JSON arrays involves creating a corresponding list in your Java model. For instance:

```java
public class PersonList {
    private List<Person> people;

    // Getter and setter
}
```

Parsing a JSON array can be done as follows:

```java
String jsonArrayString = "[{ \"name\": \"John Doe\", \"age\": 25, \"city\":
\"New York\", \"isStudent\": false, \"grades\": [85, 90, 78] }, { \"name\":
\"Jane Doe\", \"age\": 28, \"city\": \"Los Angeles\", \"isStudent\": true,
\"grades\": [92, 88, 95] }]";

PersonList personList = gson.fromJson(jsonArrayString, PersonList.class);
```

It's crucial to handle exceptions during JSON parsing to prevent crashes. Gson might throw a JsonSyntaxException if the JSON is not well-formed. Always wrap your parsing code in a try-catch block:

```java
try {
    Person person = gson.fromJson(jsonString, Person.class);
} catch (JsonSyntaxException e) {
    e.printStackTrace();
}
```

XML Parsing

XML (eXtensible Markup Language) is another commonly used data format, particularly in web services and data exchange scenarios. Android developers often encounter XML when working with APIs or dealing with data in XML format. XML parsing in Android can be accomplished using various methods, and one common approach involves using the built-in XmlPullParser class. Here's a guide on XML parsing in Android with code snippets:

Android provides the XmlPullParser interface, which is efficient and suitable for parsing XML data. The process generally involves creating an instance of XmlPullParser, iterating through the XML content, and extracting data as needed.

1. Add Permission in Manifest:

Ensure that you have the necessary internet permission in your AndroidManifest.xml if you are fetching XML data from a remote server.

```
<uses-permission android:name="android.permission.INTERNET" />
```

2. Perform XML Parsing:

Create a method for XML parsing, typically within an AsyncTask or background thread to avoid blocking the main thread. Here's a basic example:

```java
import android.util.Xml;
import org.xmlpull.v1.XmlPullParser;
import java.io.InputStream;
import java.util.ArrayList;
import java.util.List;

public class XmlParser {

    public List<Item> parse(InputStream inputStream) {
        List<Item> items = new ArrayList<>();
        XmlPullParser xmlPullParser = Xml.newPullParser();

        try {
            xmlPullParser.setInput(inputStream, null);
            int eventType = xmlPullParser.getEventType();
            Item currentItem = null;

            while (eventType != XmlPullParser.END_DOCUMENT) {
                String tagName = xmlPullParser.getName();

                switch (eventType) {
                    case XmlPullParser.START_TAG:
                        if ("item".equals(tagName)) {
                            currentItem = new Item();
                        }
                        break;

                    case XmlPullParser.TEXT:
                        if (currentItem != null) {
                            String text = xmlPullParser.getText();
                            currentItem.setContent(text);
                        }
                        break;
```

```java
                    case XmlPullParser.END_TAG:
                        if ("item".equals(tagName)) {
                            items.add(currentItem);
                            currentItem = null;
                        }
                        break;
                }

                eventType = xmlPullParser.next();
            }

        } catch (Exception e) {
            e.printStackTrace();
        }

        return items;
    }
}
```

In this example, Item is a simple Java class with a content field. Adjust the parsing logic based on the structure of your XML data.

3. Execute Parsing:

Execute the parsing operation, typically in an AsyncTask or background thread:

```java
import android.os.AsyncTask;
import java.io.InputStream;
import java.net.HttpURLConnection;
import java.net.URL;
import java.util.List;

public class XmlParsingTask extends AsyncTask<String, Void, List<Item>> {

    @Override
    protected List<Item> doInBackground(String... urls) {
        try {
            URL url = new URL(urls[0]);
            HttpURLConnection connection = (HttpURLConnection)
url.openConnection();
            InputStream inputStream = connection.getInputStream();

            XmlParser xmlParser = new XmlParser();
            return xmlParser.parse(inputStream);

        } catch (Exception e) {
            e.printStackTrace();
        }
```

```java
        return null;
    }

    @Override
    protected void onPostExecute(List<Item> items) {
        // Handle the parsed items here
    }
}
```

This AsyncTask fetches XML data from a URL and parses it using the XmlParser. Adjust the URL and handling of parsed data based on your requirements.

XML parsing in Android can vary based on the XML structure and complexity.

PART 3

Getting through Database

CHAPTER 6

INTRODUCTION TO FIREBASE

Firebase is a comprehensive mobile and web application development platform provided by Google. It offers a set of tools and services to simplify various aspects of app development, allowing developers to focus on creating innovative features rather than dealing with infrastructure complexities. Firebase encompasses a wide range of services, including real-time databases, authentication, cloud storage, hosting, and more, making it a versatile and integrated solution for building modern applications.

- Firebase is a product of Google which helps developers to build, manage, and grow their apps easily. It helps developers to build their apps faster and in a more secure way.
- No programming is required on the firebase side which makes it easy to use its features more efficiently. It provides services to android, ios, web, and unity.
- It provides cloud storage.
- It uses NoSQL for the database for the storage of data.
- Firebase, a comprehensive development platform by Google, simplifies app development with its real-time database, robust authentication, scalable cloud storage, and serverless computing through Cloud Functions.
- Developers benefit from Firebase's seamless cross-platform support, enabling the creation of responsive and collaborative applications.
- The platform's integrated ecosystem, including analytics, dynamic links, and machine learning features, fosters efficient development.
- Firebase's cost-effective pay-as-you-go model, security rules, and strong community support make it an accessible and powerful choice for building modern, scalable applications with features like real-time updates, user authentication, and cloud storage.
- Firebase has become a go-to platform for developers aiming to build scalable, feature-rich applications with a strong emphasis on real-time data synchronization, user authentication, and cloud services. Whether creating a mobile app or a web application, Firebase provides a versatile toolkit to streamline development and enhance the overall user experience.

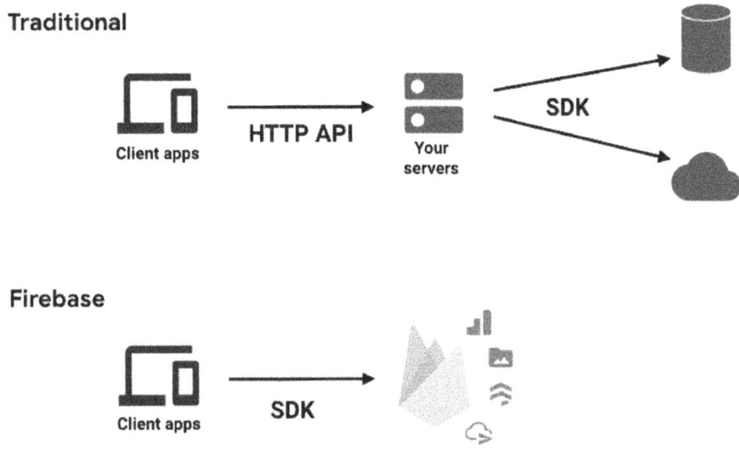

(Fig. 6.1) Traditional method v/s Firebase

History of Firebase

Firebase, initially an independent startup, was founded by James Tamplin and Andrew Lee in 2011 with the goal of providing a scalable backend infrastructure for developers. The company aimed to simplify the complexities of server-side development and offer real-time data synchronization for web and mobile applications. Firebase started as a robust API for building collaborative and synchronized apps in real-time, using a NoSQL database.

In 2014, Firebase was acquired by Google, marking a significant milestone in its evolution. The acquisition expanded Firebase's resources and integration with Google's cloud services, enhancing its capabilities. Firebase's real-time database, coupled with additional services like authentication, cloud storage, and hosting, gained popularity among developers for its simplicity and ease of use.

Over the years, Firebase continued to evolve and introduced new features, such as Cloud Functions for serverless computing, Firestore as a scalable NoSQL database, and various tools for analytics, machine learning, and dynamic links. The platform's emphasis on real-time data synchronization, coupled with Google's infrastructure, positioned Firebase as a versatile and comprehensive development platform.

Firebase's success can be attributed to its ability to address the challenges of modern app development, providing developers with a unified platform to build, deploy, and scale applications efficiently. The platform's history reflects a commitment to empowering developers with powerful tools, enabling them to focus on creating engaging user experiences without the complexities of managing backend infrastructure.

Key Components and Features of Firebase:

1. **Realtime Database:** Firebase provides a NoSQL cloud database that allows developers to store and sync data in real-time. It's particularly useful for applications requiring collaborative features and live updates.

2. **Authentication:** Firebase Authentication simplifies the user authentication process. It supports various authentication methods, including email/password, social media logins, and phone number verification.

3. **Cloud Firestore:** Firestore is a scalable and flexible NoSQL database that complements Firebase's real-time database. It's designed to handle complex data structures and supports powerful queries.

4. **Cloud Functions:** Firebase Cloud Functions enable serverless computing, allowing developers to run backend code in response to events triggered by Firebase features or HTTPS requests.

5. **Cloud Storage:** Firebase offers secure and scalable cloud storage for storing and serving user-generated content such as images, videos, and files.

6. **Hosting:** Firebase Hosting provides a fast and secure solution for deploying web apps, static content, and dynamic serverless functions. It includes features like automatic SSL deployment and CDN integration.

7. **Machine Learning:** Firebase integrates machine learning features, allowing developers to incorporate ML models into their applications without extensive expertise. This includes image labeling, language recognition, and more.

8. **Performance Monitoring:** Firebase Performance Monitoring provides insights into app performance, allowing developers to identify and address performance bottlenecks.

9. **Cloud Messaging:** Firebase Cloud Messaging (FCM) enables developers to send messages and notifications to users across various platforms, helping engage and retain users.

10. **Remote Config:** Firebase Remote Config allows developers to customize the behavior and appearance of their apps without publishing updates, providing a flexible way to experiment and optimize user experience.

11. **Dynamic Links:** Firebase Dynamic Links simplify the sharing of content across platforms and devices. They enable deep linking, helping drive user engagement.

Benefits of Using Firebase:

- **Real-Time Data Sync:** Firebase's real-time database and Firestore enable seamless data synchronization across devices, providing users with up-to-date information in real-time.

- **Scalability:** Firebase services are designed to scale with the growth of an application, ensuring performance and reliability even as user numbers increase.

- **Integrated Ecosystem:** The cohesive set of Firebase services creates a unified development experience, simplifying tasks such as authentication, database management, and cloud storage.

- **Cross-Platform Development:** Firebase supports both iOS and Android platforms, making it an ideal choice for cross-platform development. Developers can use a single codebase for multiple platforms.

- **Serverless Computing:** Firebase Cloud Functions offer serverless computing, allowing developers to execute backend code without managing servers, reducing infrastructure complexities.

Pillars of Firebase

Firebase is commonly organized into three main pillars, each addressing distinct aspects of the app development lifecycle:

1. **Build:** The "Build" pillar of Firebase focuses on providing tools and services for the actual development and creation of applications. Key features include:

    i. **Realtime Database and Firestore:** NoSQL databases for real-time data storage and synchronization.
    ii. **Authentication:** Secure user authentication with various login methods.
    iii. **Cloud Functions:** Serverless functions for event-driven backend logic.
    iv. **Storage:** It allows developers to store and serve user-generated content, such as images, videos, and other files, in a scalable and secure manner.
    v. **Firebase Hosting:** Fast and secure hosting for web apps, static content, and serverless functions.

2. **Release and Monitor:** The "Release and Monitor" pillar is dedicated to deployment, monitoring, and optimization of applications. Core features include:

    i. **Performance Monitoring:** Insights into app responsiveness and load times for performance optimization.
    ii. **Crashlytics:** Real-time crash reporting to identify and resolve issues promptly.
    iii. **App Distribution:** Streamlining app distribution to different platforms for efficient release.

3. **Engage:** The "Engage" pillar revolves around user engagement, analytics, and feedback. Notable features include:
    i. **Firebase Analytics:** Comprehensive analytics for understanding user behavior and app performance.

ii. **Cloud Messaging:** Engaging users with targeted messages and notifications.
iii. **A/B Testing:** Experimentation and optimization of app features through A/B testing.
iv. **Remote Config:** Dynamically adjusting app behavior and appearance without publishing updates.
v.   **Dynamic Links:** Simplifying user sharing and enhancing user experience with dynamic links.

These three pillars collectively provide a comprehensive solution for the entire app development lifecycle, streamlining the processes of building, releasing, monitoring, and engaging with applications. Firebase's integrated approach facilitates a seamless transition between different stages of app development.

We will discuss on each pillar of firebase respectively in the upcoming chapters.

Integrating Firebase into an Android App

Integrating Firebase into an Android app involves several steps to enable Firebase services and SDKs. Here's a concise guide on how to add Firebase to an Android app:

1. Create a Firebase Project:

- Visit the Firebase Console (https://console.firebase.google.com) and log in with your Google account.
- Click on "Add project" and follow the prompts to create a new Firebase project.
- Choose a project name and select your country or region.

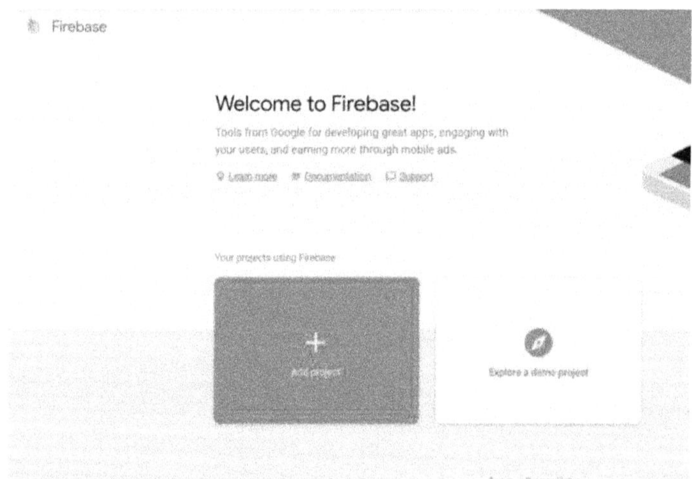

2. Register Your App with Firebase:

- After creating the project, click on "Add app" and select the Android platform.
- Enter your app's package name (e.g., "com.example.myapp") and an optional app nickname.
- Optionally, you can enable Google Analytics for your project.

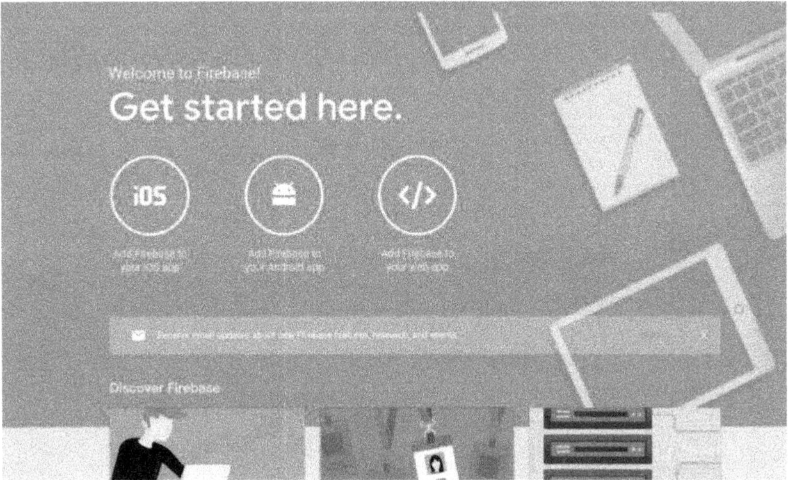

3. Download and Add the Configuration File:

- Click "Register app," and Firebase will generate a google-services.json configuration file.
- Download the file and place it in the app module of your Android project.

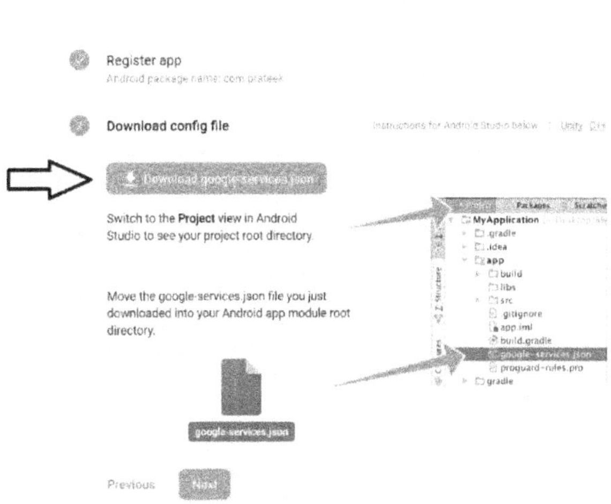

4. Add Firebase SDK to Your App:

- Open the build.gradle (Module: app) file in your Android Studio project.
- Add the Firebase SDK dependencies inside the dependencies block:

```
implementation 'com.google.firebase:firebase-auth:23.0.0'
// Add other dependencies as needed
```

- Check the Firebase documentation for the latest versions.

5. Initialize Firebase in Your App:

- Open the main Activity or the Application class in your app.
- In the onCreate method, add the following code to initialize Firebase:

```
// Add this line in your Java class
FirebaseApp.initializeApp(this);
```

6. Add Additional Firebase Services (Optional):

If you plan to use specific Firebase services (e.g., Authentication, Realtime Database), follow the additional setup instructions for those services. Adjust dependencies and initialization code accordingly.

7. Sync Gradle and Verify:

- Click "Sync Now" in Android Studio to sync your Gradle files and resolve dependencies.
- Verify the successful integration by checking the Firebase console for your app's status.

After completing these steps, your Android app is fully integrated with Firebase, and you can start using Firebase services in your application.

CHAPTER 7

BUILDING IN FIREBASE

In the "Build" phase, developers leverage these Firebase components to construct the core infrastructure, implement dynamic features, and create a solid foundation for their applications. Firebase's comprehensive suite of tools facilitates efficient and scalable application development.

Leveraging the Realtime Database and Firestore for dynamic data management, Authentication for secure user access, and Cloud Functions for event-driven logic, Firebase provides a scalable backend infrastructure. The inclusion of Cloud Firestore offers advanced querying capabilities, while Firebase ML Kit introduces machine learning features. Additionally, Firebase Hosting simplifies deployment, ensuring fast and secure hosting for various app elements. Together, these tools empower developers to create feature-rich and intelligent applications with efficiency and ease during the crucial build phase of development.

Let's have a depth understanding of the different features offered by Firebase under the Build pillar:

Realtime Database

Firebase Realtime Database is a cloud-hosted NoSQL database that allows developers to store and synchronize data in real-time across multiple clients. It is a part of the Firebase suite, offering a scalable and flexible solution for building real-time applications. Here are key features and concepts of Firebase Realtime Database:

Key Features:

1. **Real-Time Synchronization:**
   - Changes made to the data in the database are instantly propagated to all connected clients in real-time.
   - Clients receive updates automatically whenever data changes, providing a seamless and responsive user experience.

2. **NoSQL Data Model:**
   - Firebase Realtime Database uses a JSON-like data structure, allowing developers to store and retrieve data in a hierarchical format.
   - It provides flexibility in data modeling without the need for a predefined schema.

3. **Offline Support:**
   - Firebase offers offline support, allowing users to read and write data even when the device is not connected to the internet.
   - Changes made offline are synchronized with the server once the device regains connectivity.

4. **Scalability:**
   - Firebase Realtime Database scales automatically to handle a growing number of users and data.
   - The infrastructure is managed by Google Cloud, ensuring reliability and scalability.

5. **Security Rules:**
   - Developers can define security rules to control access to data, ensuring that only authorized users can read or write specific parts of the database.

- Rules can be customized based on authentication status, user IDs, and more.

Concept of Realtime Database

Firebase Realtime Database operates on fundamental concepts that define its structure and functionality.

- **Data Structure:**

At its core, the database organizes data as a JSON tree. Each node in the tree can have zero or more child nodes, creating a hierarchical structure. Every piece of data within this structure is uniquely identified by a URL, allowing for precise referencing.

- **References:**

References serve as pointers within the database, guiding developers to specific locations in the data tree. Developers leverage references for both reading and writing operations, enabling targeted interactions with distinct parts of the database.

- **Events:**

The Realtime Database responds to data changes through events, including additions, updates, or deletions. Developers can set up listeners to these events, facilitating real-time updates to the user interface based on modifications in the underlying data.

- **Transactions:**

To ensure the integrity and consistency of data updates, Firebase Realtime Database employs transactions. These transactions are crucial in scenarios where multiple clients might simultaneously attempt to modify the same data, maintaining atomicity and preventing conflicts.

In essence, these key concepts empower developers to structure data efficiently, navigate the database, respond to changes in real-time, and manage data integrity through transactions in Firebase Realtime Database.

Integrating Firebase Realtime Database

Integrating Firebase Realtime Database into an Android app allows you to store and synchronize data in real-time. Here's a guide on how to set up Firebase Realtime Database in your Android app:

1. Enable Firebase Realtime Database:

- Open the Firebase Console.
- Select your project.
- In the left menu, click on "Database" under the "Build" section.

2. Set Up Realtime Database Rules:

- Click on the "Rules" tab.
- Update the rules to control access to your database. For initial testing, you can set rules to allow read and write access to everyone:

```
{
```

```
  "rules": {
    ".read": true,
    ".write": true
  }
}
```

3. Add Firebase Realtime Database Dependency:

- Open your app's build.gradle (Module: app) file.
- Add the Realtime Database dependency:

```
implementation 'com.google.firebase:firebase-database:23.0.0'
```

4. Initialize Firebase Realtime Database:

- In your app's entry point (e.g., onCreate method of Application class or main Activity), initialize Firebase:

```
// Add this line in your Java class

FirebaseDatabase.getInstance().setPersistenceEnabled(true); // Enable
offline capabilities (optional)
```

5. Write Data to Firebase Realtime Database:

- To write data to the database, create a reference to the database and use setValue or push:

```
DatabaseReference databaseReference =
FirebaseDatabase.getInstance().getReference("your_data_path");
databaseReference.setValue("Hello, Firebase!"); // Replace with your data
```

6. Read Data from Firebase Realtime Database:

- To read data from the database, add a ValueEventListener to your database reference:

```
databaseReference.addValueEventListener(new ValueEventListener() {
    @Override
    public void onDataChange(DataSnapshot dataSnapshot) {
        // Handle data changes
        String value = dataSnapshot.getValue(String.class);
        // Do something with the retrieved data
    }

    @Override
    public void onCancelled(DatabaseError error) {
        // Handle errors
    }
});
```

7. Secure Your Database:

- As your app progresses, update database rules to control access securely.

By following these steps, you'll successfully integrate Firebase Realtime Database into your Android app, allowing real-time data synchronization and storage.

Firebase Authentication

Firebase Authentication provides a robust and secure solution for implementing user authentication in your applications. It offers several authentication methods, including email/password, phone number, Google Sign-In, Facebook Login, and more. Here's an overview of Firebase Authentication:

Key Features:

1. **Multiple Authentication Providers:** Firebase supports various authentication providers, allowing users to sign in using their preferred method. This includes email/password, phone number, Google, Facebook, Twitter, and more.

2. **Easy Integration:** Integration with Firebase Authentication is seamless and well-documented, making it straightforward for developers to implement authentication features into their applications.

3. **Secure Password Handling:** For email/password authentication, Firebase automatically handles password storage and security. Passwords are hashed and salted, ensuring a high level of security.

4. **Phone Number Authentication:** Firebase Authentication provides a simple yet powerful phone number authentication method. Users receive a verification code via SMS for secure login.

5. **Third-Party Provider Integration:** Integration with third-party authentication providers like Google and Facebook is simplified, allowing users to sign in with their existing credentials from these platforms.

6. **Custom Authentication System:** Developers can implement custom authentication systems, providing flexibility for unique user authentication requirements.

Authentication Flow:

- **User Registration:** Users register by providing their credentials, such as email and password, or other applicable information based on the chosen authentication method.

- **User Sign-In:** Once registered, users can sign in using their credentials. Firebase handles the authentication process, verifying the user's identity.

- **Password Recovery:** Firebase Authentication includes features for password recovery, allowing users to reset their passwords securely.

- **Multi-Factor Authentication (MFA):** For enhanced security, Firebase supports Multi-Factor Authentication, requiring users to verify their identity through multiple steps.

Security Rules

Firebase Authentication is complemented by Firebase Security Rules, which allow developers to define access control policies. These rules specify who can access different parts of the database based on user authentication status, email domains, or custom claims.

In summary, Firebase Authentication provides a comprehensive and secure solution for implementing user authentication, ensuring that only authorized users can access the features and data within your application.

Different Authentication Method

Firebase Authentication supports various methods for user authentication, allowing developers to choose the approach that best suits their application and user experience. Here are some of the key authentication methods provided by Firebase:

1. Email/Password Authentication: Users can create an account using their email address and a password. Firebase securely stores and manages these credentials.

Implementation Steps:

i.   **Initialize Firebase:** Start by initializing the Firebase SDK in your application.
ii. **Create UI Components:** Design and implement UI components for user registration and sign-in.
iii. **User Registration:** When a user wants to create an account, they provide their email address and choose a password.
iv. **Firebase Authentication SDK:** Use the Firebase Authentication SDK to create a new user account by passing the email and password.

```
FirebaseAuth.getInstance().createUserWithEmailAndPassword(email,
password)
    .addOnCompleteListener(this, new OnCompleteListener<AuthResult>() {
        @Override
        public void onComplete(@NonNull Task<AuthResult> task) {
            if (task.isSuccessful()) {
                // User registration successful
            } else {
                // Registration failed, handle the error
            }
        }
    });
```

v.   **User Sign-In:** For subsequent sign-ins, users enter their registered email and password.

```
FirebaseAuth.getInstance().signInWithEmailAndPassword(email, password)
    .addOnCompleteListener(this, new OnCompleteListener<AuthResult>() {
        @Override
        public void onComplete(@NonNull Task<AuthResult> task) {
            if (task.isSuccessful()) {

                // User sign-in successful

            } else {

                // Sign-in failed, handle the error

            }
        }
```

```
});
```

vi.   **Password Recovery:** Firebase provides a password recovery mechanism. If a user forgets their password, they can initiate a password reset.

```
FirebaseAuth.getInstance().sendPasswordResetEmail(email)
    .addOnCompleteListener(new OnCompleteListener<Void>() {
        @Override
        public void onComplete(@NonNull Task<Void> task) {
            if (task.isSuccessful()) {

                // Password reset email sent successfully

            } else {

                // Password reset failed, handle the error

            }
        }
    });
```

vii.   **User State Management:** Implement logic to manage the authentication state (signed in or signed out) based on user actions.

2. Phone Number Authentication: Users can sign in using their phone number. Firebase sends a verification code via SMS for secure authentication.

Implementation Steps:

i.   **Initialize Firebase:** Begin by initializing the Firebase SDK in your Android application.
ii.   **Create UI Components:** Design and implement the necessary UI components for phone number input and verification.
iii.   **Phone Number Verification:** When a user enters their phone number, Firebase sends a verification code via SMS to the provided number.

```
PhoneAuthProvider.getInstance().verifyPhoneNumber(
    phoneNumber,          // Phone number to verify
    60,                   // Timeout duration
    TimeUnit.SECONDS,     // Unit of timeout
    this,                 // Activity (for callback binding)
    callbacks);           // OnVerificationStateChangedCallbacks
```

iv.   **Verification Callbacks:** Implement callbacks to handle verification success, failure, and other states.

```
PhoneAuthProvider.OnVerificationStateChangedCallbacks callbacks =
    new PhoneAuthProvider.OnVerificationStateChangedCallbacks() {
        @Override
```

```java
        public void onVerificationCompleted(PhoneAuthCredential credential)
{
            // Auto-retrieval or instant verification completed successfully
            signInWithPhoneAuthCredential(credential);
        }

        @Override
        public void onVerificationFailed(FirebaseException e) {
            // Verification failed, handle the error
        }

        // Other callback methods for different states (e.g., code sent, code
resend)
    };
```

v.   **Sign In with Phone Auth Credential:** After successful verification, sign in using the obtained PhoneAuthCredential.

```java
private void signInWithPhoneAuthCredential(PhoneAuthCredential credential)
{
    FirebaseAuth.getInstance().signInWithCredential(credential)
        .addOnCompleteListener(this, new OnCompleteListener<AuthResult>() {
            @Override
            public void onComplete(@NonNull Task<AuthResult> task) {
                if (task.isSuccessful()) {

                    // Phone number authentication successful

                } else {

                    // Authentication failed, handle the error

                }
            }
        });
}
```

3. Google Sign-In: Users can sign in with their Google credentials. Firebase integrates seamlessly with Google Sign-In for quick and easy authentication.

Implementation Steps:

i.   **Initialize Firebase:** Begin by initializing the Firebase SDK in your Android application.

ii.   **Configure OAuth Consent Screen:** Set up the OAuth Consent Screen on the Google Cloud Console. This is where you define the information that will be presented to users when they sign in.

iii.   **Enable Google Sign-In:** Enable Google Sign-In in the Firebase console, and add your app's digital fingerprint to the project settings.

iv.   **Add Google Sign-In Button:** Design and include the Google Sign-In button in your app's UI.

```
<com.google.android.gms.common.SignInButton
    android:id="@+id/google_sign_in_button"
    android:layout_width="wrap_content"
    android:layout_height="wrap_content" />
```

v.   **Configure GoogleSignInOptions:** Specify the sign-in options, such as requesting the user's email address and profile.

```
GoogleSignInOptions gso = new
GoogleSignInOptions.Builder(GoogleSignInOptions.DEFAULT_SIGN_IN)
    .requestIdToken(getString(R.string.default_web_client_id))
    .requestEmail()
    .build();
```

vi.   **Initialize GoogleSignInClient:** Create an instance of GoogleSignInClient using the configured GoogleSignInOptions.

```
GoogleSignInClient mGoogleSignInClient = GoogleSignIn.getClient(this, gso);
```

vii.   **Start Google Sign-In Flow:** Trigger the Google Sign-In process when the user clicks the Sign-In button.

```
Intent signInIntent = mGoogleSignInClient.getSignInIntent();
startActivityForResult(signInIntent, RC_SIGN_IN);
```

viii.   **Handle Sign-In Result:** Handle the result of the Google Sign-In process in the onActivityResult method.

```
@Override
protected void onActivityResult(int requestCode, int resultCode, Intent
data) {
    super.onActivityResult(requestCode, resultCode, data);
    if (requestCode == RC_SIGN_IN) {
        Task<GoogleSignInAccount> task =
GoogleSignIn.getSignedInAccountFromIntent(data);
        handleSignInResult(task);
    }
}
```

ix.   **Handle Successful Sign-In:** If the sign-in is successful, obtain the user's information and update the UI accordingly.

```
private void handleSignInResult(Task<GoogleSignInAccount> completedTask) {

    try {

        GoogleSignInAccount account = completedTask.getResult(ApiException.class);

        // Signed in successfully, update UI
```

```
} catch (ApiException e) {

    // Sign in failed, handle the error

}
```

}

x.   **User State Management:** Implement logic to manage the authentication state (signed in or signed out) based on user actions.

4. Social Media Logins: Firebase supports authentication through various social media platforms, including:

- **Facebook Login:** Users can sign in with their Facebook credentials.
- **Twitter Login:** Authentication through Twitter accounts.
- **GitHub Login:** Users can use their GitHub accounts for authentication.

5. Anonymous Authentication: Users can access certain features without creating a full account. Firebase assigns an anonymous identifier to these users.

6. Custom Authentication System: Developers can implement custom authentication systems if their application requires specific user authentication logic.

7. Multi-Factor Authentication (MFA): For enhanced security, Firebase supports Multi-Factor Authentication. Users must provide multiple forms of identification for access.

8. OAuth Providers: Firebase supports OAuth providers, allowing users to sign in using their accounts from various platforms, such as:

- Microsoft
- Apple
- Yahoo

Firebase Storage

Firebase Storage is a cloud-based storage service provided by Firebase, a comprehensive mobile and web application development platform by Google. It allows developers to store and serve user-generated content, such as images, videos, and other files, in a scalable and secure manner. Firebase Storage is particularly useful for mobile and web applications that require efficient handling of media assets. Here's an overview of Firebase Storage:

- Firebase Storage organizes data into "buckets," which are top-level containers similar to folders in a file system. Each Firebase project has a default bucket, and developers can create additional buckets if needed.
- Files stored in Firebase Storage are referred to as "objects." Each object has a unique path within a bucket, similar to a file path in a traditional file system.
- Firebase Storage uses security rules to control access to files. These rules specify who can read or write to specific paths within the storage. This ensures that only authorized users can interact with certain files.

Implementation Steps:

1. **Initialize Firebase Storage:** Begin by adding the Firebase Storage dependency to your app's build.gradle file.

```
implementation 'com.google.firebase:firebase-storage:23.0.0'
```

2. **Initialize Firebase Storage in your app.**

```
FirebaseStorage storage = FirebaseStorage.getInstance();
```

3. **Upload a File:** To upload a file to Firebase Storage, you create a reference to the desired location (path) and use the putFile method.

```
StorageReference storageRef = storage.getReference();
StorageReference imageRef = storageRef.child("images/example.jpg");

Uri file = Uri.fromFile(new File("path/to/local/file.jpg"));
UploadTask uploadTask = imageRef.putFile(file);
```

4. **Download a File:** To download a file, create a reference to the file and use the getDownloadUrl method.

```
StorageReference imageRef = storageRef.child("images/example.jpg");

imageRef.getDownloadUrl().addOnSuccessListener(uri -> {

    // Handle the download URL

});
```

5. **Delete a File:** To delete a file, create a reference to the file and use the delete method.

```
StorageReference imageRef = storageRef.child("images/example.jpg");

imageRef.delete().addOnSuccessListener(aVoid -> {

    // File deleted successfully

});
```

6. **Security Rules:** Configure security rules to control access to your storage. For example, you can set rules to allow only authenticated users to upload or download files.

```
service firebase.storage {
  match /b/{bucket}/o {
    match /{allPaths=**} {
      allow read, write: if request.auth != null;
    }
  }
}
```

7. **Error Handling:** Implement error handling for upload, download, or deletion operations to provide a smooth user experience.

Cloud Functions

Firebase Cloud Functions allow developers to run backend code in response to events triggered by Firebase features and HTTPS requests. Cloud Functions offer a serverless solution for executing code without managing server infrastructure. Here's an overview of Firebase Cloud Functions:

- Firebase Cloud Functions follow the serverless computing model, allowing developers to write and deploy code without managing servers. Google Cloud Platform hosts and scales the functions automatically.
- Functions are triggered by specific events in Firebase products, such as changes in Firestore, new user sign-ups with Firebase Authentication, or file uploads to Firebase Storage. Developers can define functions to respond to these events.
- Cloud Functions use the Node.js runtime environment. Developers write functions using JavaScript or TypeScript. The functions are deployed as individual units that execute independently.
- Functions are deployed using the Firebase CLI. Each deployed function receives a unique URL. Firebase maintains versioning, allowing developers to roll back to previous versions if needed.
- In addition to event-triggered functions, developers can create HTTP functions that respond to HTTP requests. This is useful for building APIs, webhooks, or handling other HTTP-related tasks.
- Developers can use npm (Node Package Manager) to manage dependencies for Cloud Functions. This allows the use of external libraries and tools within the functions.
- Cloud Functions can execute asynchronously. For example, developers can perform background tasks, send notifications, or update data in Firestore after an event is triggered.

CHAPTER 8

ENGAGING WITH FIREBASE

ngaging with Firebase involves leveraging a suite of tools and strategies to enhance user interaction, deliver personalized content, and gain valuable insights into user behavior. Firebase offers a multifaceted approach to user engagement, and here are key components and strategies for effective engagement:

Firebase Cloud Messaging (FCM) serves as a pivotal tool for sending push notifications to users' devices. By seamlessly integrating FCM, developers can send targeted notifications, ensuring effective communication with users on both Android and iOS platforms. This facilitates real-time communication and keeps users informed and engaged.

Firebase Remote Config provides the ability to dynamically configure app settings without the need for releasing new app versions. This allows developers to tailor the app experience for different user segments, adapting content or behavior based on specific parameters defined in the Remote Config dashboard.

In-App Messaging is another powerful Firebase feature that enables the display of targeted messages within the app. This feature facilitates communication with users while they are actively using the app, delivering relevant and personalized content based on user behavior or predefined events.

Firebase Dynamic Links are deep links that play a crucial role in driving user engagement. These links operate across different platforms and devices, providing a seamless and personalized user experience by directing users to specific content or features within the app.

Firebase Analytics is an essential tool for gaining insights into user behavior, demographics, and engagement. By integrating the Firebase Analytics SDK into the app, developers can understand how users interact with the app, enabling data-driven decision-making for continuous improvement.

A/B Testing with Firebase allows developers to experiment with different app configurations to optimize user engagement. By testing variations of features, designs, or messages, developers can make informed decisions based on real user data, ensuring continuous enhancement of the app.

User feedback mechanisms are crucial for understanding user satisfaction and addressing issues promptly. Firebase offers tools like Crashlytics for crash reporting and facilitates the implementation of feedback forms or links to Firebase Cloud Functions for gathering user feedback directly within the app.

By combining these Firebase features, developers can create a holistic and engaging app experience. The ability to communicate effectively with users, personalize content, and continuously optimize the app based on real-time insights contributes to sustained user satisfaction and app growth.

Firebase Cloud Messaging

Firebase Cloud Messaging (FCM) is a robust cloud solution provided by Firebase for enabling effective communication between server applications and mobile devices. FCM serves as a reliable and efficient push notification service, allowing developers to send messages and notifications to users on both Android and iOS platforms. Here's a detailed explanation of Firebase Cloud Messaging and how it works:

Key Features:

1. **Cross-Platform Support:** FCM supports both Android and iOS, making it a versatile solution for developers targeting multiple platforms.

2. **Reliable Message Delivery:** FCM ensures the reliable and timely delivery of messages to devices, even in challenging network conditions.

3. **Notification Types:** Developers can send different types of notifications, including basic notifications, data messages, and even notification messages that can contain both.

4. **Topics and Device Groups:** FCM allows developers to send messages to devices subscribed to specific topics or belonging to device groups, enabling targeted communication.

5. **Cloud-to-Device and Device-to-Cloud Messaging:** FCM facilitates bidirectional messaging, allowing devices to send messages to the server, creating a dynamic and interactive communication model.

How FCM Works:

1. **Client Registration:** The mobile app registers with FCM, and the FCM server provides a unique registration token for the device.

2. **Server Sends a Message:** The app server sends a message to the FCM server, specifying the target device or devices using their registration tokens.

3. **Message Routing:** FCM routes the message to the target devices based on the specified criteria, such as registration tokens, topics, or device groups.

4. **Message Delivery:** The FCM server delivers the message to the target devices via the appropriate push notification service (Firebase Cloud Messaging for Android or Apple Push Notification Service for iOS).

5. **Client-Side Handling:** The mobile app receives the message, and developers can define how the app behaves in response to the received message, such as displaying a notification, updating content, or triggering specific actions.

Use Cases:

- **Push Notifications:** FCM is widely used for sending push notifications to keep users informed about updates, messages, or events related to the app.

- **Real-Time Updates:** Apps can utilize FCM to deliver real-time updates, ensuring users receive the latest information without manual refresh.

- **Marketing Campaigns:** FCM supports targeted messaging, allowing developers to send personalized notifications based on user behavior or demographics.

- **In-App Messaging:** FCM can be integrated with in-app messaging to enhance user engagement by displaying relevant content or promotions.

By incorporating Firebase Cloud Messaging into their apps, developers can enhance user engagement, deliver timely information, and create a more dynamic and interactive user experience.

How to implement FCM?

To implement Firebase Cloud Messaging (FCM) in your Android app, you need to perform several steps. Here is a basic guide on how to implement FCM in an Android app using Java:

Step 1: Set up Firebase Project (As instructed in Chapter 6)

Step 2: Add Dependencies

- Add the necessary dependencies in your app-level build.gradle file:

```
implementation 'com.google.firebase:firebase-messaging:23.0.0'
```

Step 3: Configure FCM in the App

- Add the following code to your AndroidManifest.xml file:

```xml
<service
    android:name=".MyFirebaseMessagingService">
    <intent-filter>
        <action android:name="com.google.firebase.MESSAGING_EVENT" />
    </intent-filter>
</service>
```

Step 4: Create FirebaseMessagingService Class

- Create a class that extends FirebaseMessagingService to handle incoming messages:

```java
import com.google.firebase.messaging.FirebaseMessagingService;
import com.google.firebase.messaging.RemoteMessage;

public class MyFirebaseMessagingService extends
FirebaseMessagingService {

    @Override
    public void onMessageReceived(RemoteMessage remoteMessage) {

        // Handle incoming messages here
        // You can display a notification, update UI, etc.

    }

    @Override
    public void onNewToken(String token) {

        // Called when a new token is generated
```

```
        // You might want to send this token to your server for future
use


    }
}
```

Step 5: Handle Messages in Your App

- Update the onMessageReceived method in your MyFirebaseMessagingService class to handle incoming messages. You can display notifications, update the UI, or perform any desired action.

```
@Override
public void onMessageReceived(RemoteMessage remoteMessage) {

    // Handle incoming messages

    if (remoteMessage.getData().size() > 0) {

        // Handle data messages
        // You can extract data from remoteMessage.getData()

    }

    if (remoteMessage.getNotification() != null) {

        // Handle notification messages
        // You can display a notification using NotificationCompat

    }
}
```

Step 6: Obtain FCM Token

- To obtain the FCM token, you can use the following code in your MainActivity or any other relevant class:

```
FirebaseInstanceId.getInstance().getInstanceId().addOnCompleteListener
(task -> {
    if (task.isSuccessful()) {
        String token = task.getResult().getToken();

        // Now you have the FCM token

    }
});
```

Step 7: Send Test Message

- Using the Firebase Console, you can send a test message to your app to verify that the setup is working.

Firebase Remote Config

Firebase Remote Config is a powerful tool provided by Firebase that enables developers to dynamically configure and customize the behavior and appearance of their apps without requiring a new app release. This feature allows developers to fine-tune app parameters remotely, ensuring a personalized and adaptive user experience. Here's an overview of Firebase Remote Config and how it works:

Key Features:

1. **Dynamic Configuration:** Firebase Remote Config allows developers to define parameters such as feature flags, text strings, and other settings that can be modified remotely without the need for app updates.

2. **A/B Testing:** Developers can use Remote Config to perform A/B testing by experimenting with different configurations on different user segments. This helps in understanding user preferences and optimizing app features.

3. **Conditional Parameters:** Configurations can be set based on conditions such as app version, device type, language, or any other user attributes, enabling precise targeting of specific user groups.

4. **Instant Rollback:** In case of issues with a new configuration, developers can instantly roll back to the previous configuration without requiring a new app release.

5. **Audience Targeting:** Firebase Remote Config integrates with Firebase Analytics, allowing developers to target specific user segments based on analytics data, ensuring personalized experiences for different user groups.

How Firebase Remote Config Works:

1. **Initialization:** The app initializes Firebase Remote Config, fetching the default configurations defined in the app.

2. **Fetch Configurations:** The app requests updated configurations from the Firebase Remote Config server.

3. **Server-Side Configuration:** Developers can use the Firebase console to set configurations on the server side. These configurations are then fetched by the app.

4. **Conditional Evaluation:** Configurations can be conditionally applied based on specified criteria such as user attributes, language, or device type.

5. **Activation:** Once fetched, the updated configurations are activated in the app, and the app adapts its behavior based on the new settings.

6. **Caching:** The fetched configurations are cached locally, reducing the need for frequent network requests and ensuring optimal performance.

Use Cases:

- **Feature Rollouts:** Gradual rollout of new features or changes to assess their impact on user engagement and app performance.

- **Text Customization:** Dynamic customization of text strings, allowing for language-specific content or instant updates to promotional messages.

- **Behavioral Tweaks:** Adjusting app behavior, UI elements, or default settings based on user segments or A/B testing results.

- **Promotional Campaigns:** Instantly changing promotional banners, discounts, or offers without requiring a new app release.

By leveraging Firebase Remote Config, developers can maintain greater control over their app's behavior, respond to user feedback in real-time, and deliver a personalized and adaptive user experience.

Dynamic Links

Firebase Dynamic Links are a powerful feature that enables developers to create dynamic, smart URLs that can adapt to different platforms and scenarios. These links direct users to specific content or features within a mobile application. Firebase Dynamic Links work across both Android and iOS platforms, making them a versatile tool for improving user experiences and engagement. Here's a breakdown of their key features and how they work:

1. **Cross-Platform Compatibility:**
   - Firebase Dynamic Links are designed to seamlessly work on both Android and iOS devices.
   - The same link can intelligently open the corresponding content in the respective app store, redirecting users to the correct app version based on their device.

2. **Adaptable Behavior:**
   - Dynamic Links can be configured to behave differently based on various conditions.
   - For example, if a user doesn't have the app installed, the link can redirect them to the app store, and after installation, open the app to the specified content.

3. **Deep Linking:**
   - Firebase Dynamic Links support deep linking, allowing users to be directed to specific pages or content within an app.
   - This enhances user experience by taking them directly to the content of interest rather than just launching the app's main screen.

4. **Custom Parameters:**
   - Developers can include custom parameters in Dynamic Links, enabling them to carry data that the app can use upon launch.
   - This feature is beneficial for personalization and tailoring the user experience based on contextual information.

5. **Short Links:**
   - Firebase provides the option to create short links, making the URLs more shareable and user-friendly.

- Short links are particularly useful for sharing in contexts with character limitations, such as social media or QR codes.

6. **Tracking and Analytics:**
   - Firebase Dynamic Links offer analytics to track link clicks and user interactions.
   - Developers can gain insights into how users are engaging with their links, helping them make data-driven decisions.

7. **Fallback URLs:**
   - In cases where the app is not installed, developers can provide a fallback URL that directs users to a web page with similar content.
   - This ensures a smooth experience for users who may not have the app installed.

8. **Easy Integration with Firebase Services:**
   - Dynamic Links seamlessly integrate with other Firebase services, such as Firebase Analytics, to provide a comprehensive solution for app development and user engagement.

Handle Dynamic Links

In your activity or wherever you want to handle the dynamic link, use the following code snippet:

```
FirebaseDynamicLinks.getInstance()
    .getDynamicLink(getIntent())
    .addOnSuccessListener(this, pendingDynamicLinkData -> {
        // Handle the dynamic link data
        if (pendingDynamicLinkData != null) {
            Uri deepLink = pendingDynamicLinkData.getLink();
            // Use deepLink to navigate to the relevant content
        }
    })
    .addOnFailureListener(this, e -> {
        // Handle any errors
    });
```

Crashlytics

Firebase Crashlytics is a robust crash reporting tool that allows developers to gain insights into app crashes in real-time. By seamlessly integrating with Firebase, Crashlytics offers a comprehensive solution for identifying and addressing issues that lead to application crashes.

When implementing Firebase Crashlytics in an Android app, the first step is to create a Firebase project through the Firebase Console. Following this, the Crashlytics SDK needs to be added to the project's dependencies. This can be achieved by including the appropriate dependency in the app-level build.gradle file. Once the SDK is added, developers must initialize Firebase and enable Crashlytics in the application's entry point, typically in the Application class or main activity.

- Testing Crashlytics involves intentionally triggering a crash in the app, such as by calling `FirebaseCrashlytics.getInstance().crash()`. This allows developers to verify that crash reports are being captured and sent to the Firebase Console. It's essential to set `setCrashlyticsCollectionEnabled` to true during initialization to ensure that crash data is collected.

- In addition to capturing uncaught exceptions automatically, developers can use Crashlytics to log caught exceptions. This involves wrapping potentially problematic code in a try-catch block and using `FirebaseCrashlytics.getInstance().recordException(e)` to record the caught exception.

- The Firebase Console serves as the central hub for analyzing crash reports. Developers can navigate to the "Crashlytics" section to access detailed information about crashes, view trends, and prioritize issues based on the number of affected users. The console provides a user-friendly interface for monitoring the health of the app and facilitating prompt issue resolution.

- When dealing with release builds, developers need to ensure that Crashlytics works seamlessly. Firebase usually handles this automatically if the configuration file (google-services.json) is correctly added to the project. Additionally, if the app employs code obfuscation through Proguard, it is crucial to configure Proguard to work harmoniously with Crashlytics.

Add Firebase Crashlytics SDK:

- Open your app-level build.gradle file. Add the following dependency for Crashlytics:

```
implementation 'com.google.firebase:firebase-crashlytics:18.0.0'
```

Enable Crashlytics:

- In your Application class or main activity, initialize Firebase and enable Crashlytics:

```java
import android.app.Application;
import com.google.firebase.FirebaseApp;
import com.google.firebase.crashlytics.FirebaseCrashlytics;

public class YourApplication extends Application {

    @Override
    public void onCreate() {
        super.onCreate();
        FirebaseApp.initializeApp(this);

FirebaseCrashlytics.getInstance().setCrashlyticsCollectionEnabled(true);
    }
}
```

Test Crash Reporting:

- To test Crashlytics, force a crash in your app. For example, add the following code:

```java
FirebaseCrashlytics.getInstance().crash();
```

- Run your app, and you should see the crash reported in the Firebase Console.

Handle Uncaught Exceptions:

- Crashlytics automatically captures uncaught exceptions. However, if you want to log caught exceptions, use the following code:

```
try {
    // Your code that may throw an exception
} catch (Exception e) {
    FirebaseCrashlytics.getInstance().recordException(e);
}
```

View Crash Reports:

- Navigate to the Firebase Console, select your project, and go to "Crashlytics" in the left menu.
- Here, you can view detailed crash reports, analyze trends, and prioritize issues based on the number of affected users.

Firebase Analytics

Firebase Analytics serves as an essential tool for app developers, offering a comprehensive and free analytics solution to gain insights into user behavior. By tracking various user interactions and events, developers can make informed decisions to enhance the overall user experience.

One of its key features is event tracking, allowing developers to log events that signify user actions within the app, such as button clicks, purchases, or sign-ups. Events can be customized and categorized based on the specific needs of the app.

- Firebase Analytics also provides the ability to define user properties, enabling segmentation of the user base. This segmentation can be based on factors like subscription status or geographic location, offering a more targeted approach to analyzing user data.
- User engagement metrics, such as active users, retention, and engagement over time, can be monitored through Firebase Analytics. This information helps developers understand user behavior, including how often users return to the app and the duration of their engagement.
- Conversion tracking is another crucial aspect, allowing developers to measure the effectiveness of the app in achieving specific goals, like completing a tutorial or making a purchase. Funnel analysis provides insights into user journeys, identifying potential drop-off points and enabling optimization of user flows.
- Audiences can be created based on user behavior or attributes, facilitating targeted communication with specific user groups. Firebase Analytics also supports attribution, helping developers understand the sources of app installs and assess the impact of marketing efforts.
- Integration with other Firebase services enhances the development platform's capabilities. Firebase Analytics seamlessly works with services like Firebase Crashlytics, Remote Config, and Dynamic Links, providing a holistic approach to app development.

How to initialize Firebase Analytics?

```
import com.google.firebase.analytics.FirebaseAnalytics;

// ...
```

```java
public class YourApplication extends Application {

    @Override
    public void onCreate() {
        super.onCreate();
        FirebaseAnalytics.getInstance(this);
    }
}
```

How to log events using Firebase Analytics?

```java
Bundle params = new Bundle();
params.putString(FirebaseAnalytics.Param.ITEM_ID, "button_click");
params.putString(FirebaseAnalytics.Param.ITEM_NAME, "Button Clicked");
FirebaseAnalytics.getInstance(context).logEvent(FirebaseAnalytics.Event.SEL
ECT_CONTENT, params);
```

After implementing Firebase Analytics, you can view analytics data in the Firebase Console. Navigate to your project, select "Analytics" from the left menu, and explore the available reports and insights.

PART 4

App Launchpad & Practical Guide

CHAPTER 9

LAUNCHING AN APP TO PLAY STORE

Publishing an app on the Google Play Store is a multi-step process that involves careful preparation and adherence to guidelines set by Google. The journey begins with setting up a Google Play Console account. This requires creating or logging into a Google account and paying a one-time registration fee. Once the developer account is established, the Google Play Console becomes the central dashboard for managing the app's presence on the Play Store.

Before embarking on the submission process, it is crucial to ensure that the app is polished and ready for public consumption. This includes thorough testing on different devices and screen sizes to guarantee a smooth user experience. The developer must also familiarize themselves with the Play Store policies and guidelines to avoid potential issues during the review process.

With the app prepared and the Play Console ready, the next step involves creating a compelling store listing. This involves crafting an engaging app title, writing a descriptive and informative summary, and selecting visually appealing screenshots and graphics. Clear and concise communication is key in attracting potential users and setting proper expectations.

Once the store listing is perfected, decisions regarding the app's pricing and distribution must be made. Developers can choose whether their app will be free or paid, and they can select the countries where it will be available. This step is critical in reaching the desired target audience and maximizing the app's potential reach.

The heart of the publishing process lies in uploading the APK (Android Package) file. This file encapsulates the app's code, resources, and assets. Developers use Android Studio or other relevant tools to generate a signed APK, ensuring it is securely signed with a keystore. Versioning and handling updates are also vital aspects at this stage.

Content rating and policy adherence come into play next. Developers complete a content rating questionnaire to categorize their app appropriately. It is essential to provide a transparent privacy policy, especially if the app collects personal or sensitive information.

The final stretch involves the review and publication of the app. After submission, Google reviews the app to ensure it complies with its policies. This process may take anywhere from a few hours to several days. Once the review is complete and the app is approved, developers can proudly hit the "Publish" button. The app is now live on the Play Store, ready to be discovered and downloaded by users worldwide.

Post-publication, developers should monitor their app's performance, engage with user feedback, and consider promotional strategies to enhance visibility. Regular updates and responsiveness to user needs contribute to a successful and well-maintained app presence on the Google Play Store.

Understanding the App Publishing Landscape

This section of the book aims to demystify the process of getting your Android app onto the Google Play Store. Publishing an app involves several crucial steps, and understanding the landscape is the first key to success.

Section 1: The Google Play Console

The Google Play Console is your central hub for managing your app's presence on the Play Store. Learn how to set up your developer account, navigate the console interface, and explore the essential tools it provides. From app creation to analytics, the Console is your command center.

Section 2: Preparing Your App for Publication

Before diving into the Play Store, ensure your app is polished and ready for the world. This section covers best practices for app design, testing strategies, and optimizing performance. We'll discuss how to handle different screen sizes, resolutions, and provide tips on creating a stellar user experience.

Section 3: Creating a Compelling Store Listing

Your app's store listing is the face it presents to potential users. Dive into crafting an engaging app title, writing a compelling description, selecting eye-catching visuals, and choosing the right category. Learn how to highlight your app's unique features to attract and retain users.

Section 4: Pricing and Distribution

Determine whether your app will be free or paid and choose the countries where it will be available. We'll explore different pricing models and distribution strategies to help you reach your target audience effectively.

Section 5: Uploading Your APK

The APK (Android Package) is the core of your app. Understand the steps to generate a signed APK from Android Studio and seamlessly upload it to the Play Console. Learn about versioning, signing, and handling updates to keep your app current.

Section 6: Content Rating and Policies

Navigate the Play Store's content rating system to ensure your app aligns with appropriate audiences. Familiarize yourself with Google's policies to avoid common pitfalls that could lead to rejection. We'll delve into privacy concerns and the importance of providing a transparent privacy policy.

Section 7: Review and Publication

Explore what happens during the review process, from submission to publication. Learn how to handle potential issues that may arise during review and strategies to expedite the process. Finally, hit the "Publish" button and celebrate the moment your app goes live!

Generating Signed Apk File

Step 1: Sign in to your Google Account as shown below. If you are already logged in move to the next step.

Step 2: From the toolbar, click on the 'Build' option and select the 'Generate Signed Bundle / APK.

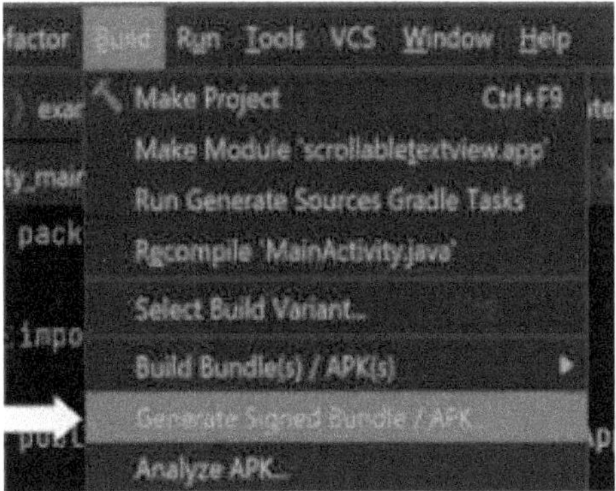

Step 3: Now on the appeared pop-up window select 'APK' in the radio button as shown in the image below. Then, click on the 'Next' button.

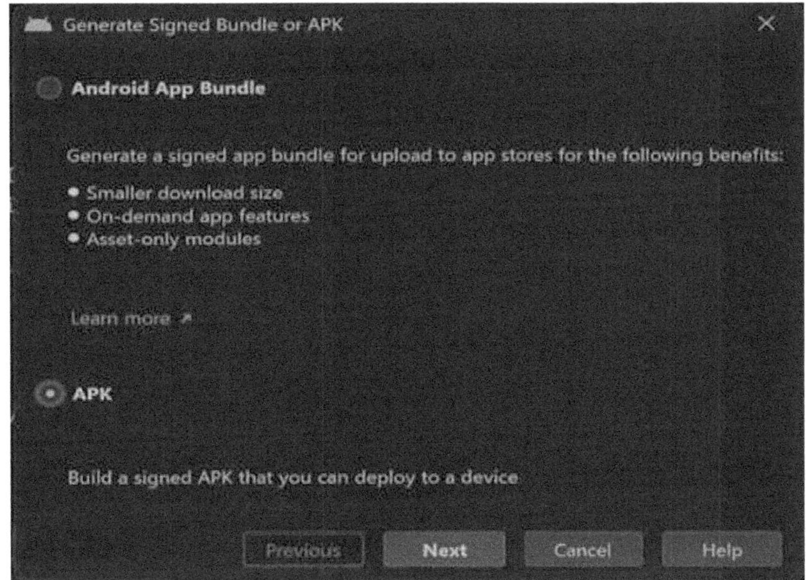

Step 4: Now Create a new KeyStore credential for your App by clicking on "Create New".

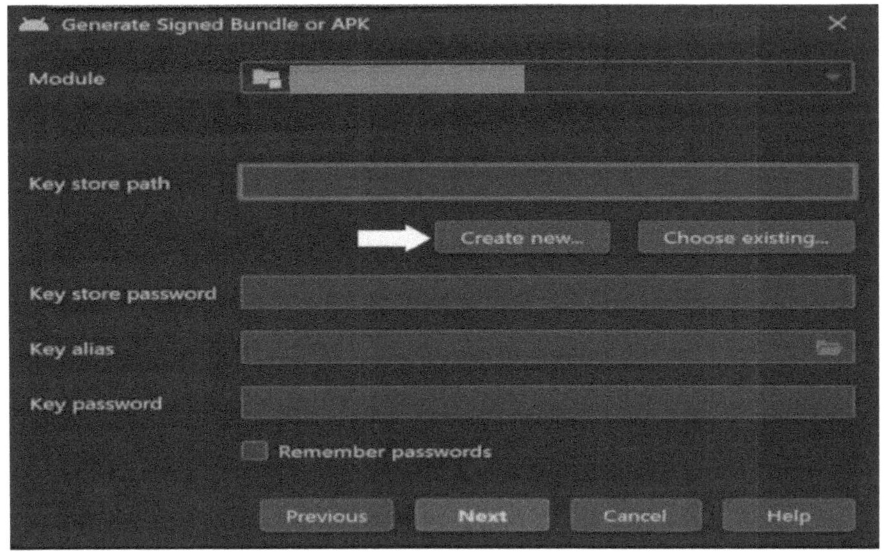

Step 5: In 'New Key Store', browse a 'Key store path' by clicking on the Folder icon as shown. Then, provide a 'Password' and 'Confirm' password. Now, on the 'Key' section, provide an 'Alias:' or go with the already provided one.

After that enter a 'Password' and 'Confirm' password. After that, you can move on to the 'Certificate' section. here, provide your 'First and Last Name'. Enter your address details. After you have provided the required details, click on the 'OK'.

Step 6: You will see the path for your KeyStore with the password you gave. Click on next.

Step 7: On the pop-up window select Release and end the process by clicking on Finish as shown below.

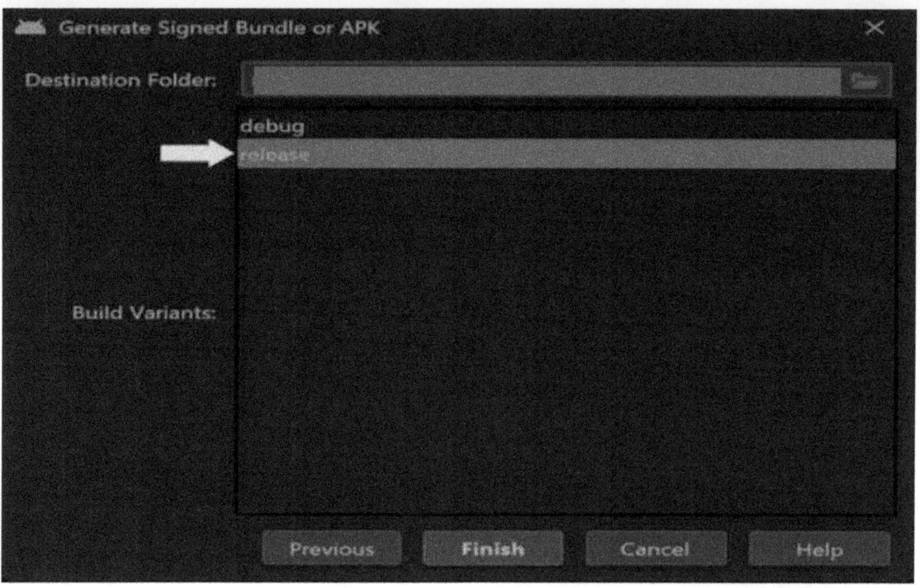

Output:

Android Studio will take a few minutes to generate the APK file. Once the APK file build is complete, you'll receive a notification on the bottom right corner of your screen. Select Locate and you will find the APK file location. The Signed APK file is by default named app-release.apk. You will find it in the project folder in the app/release directory.

Setting up Google Play Console

Step 1: Create a Google Play Developer Account

To start, visit the Google Play Console website (https://play.google.com/apps/publish/) and sign in with your Google account or create a new one if you don't have an account. After signing in, you'll need to agree to the Developer Distribution Agreement and pay a one-time registration fee, which was $25 as of my last update in 2022.

Step 2: Set Up Your Developer Profile

Once your account is set up, complete your developer profile by providing relevant information. This includes details about yourself or your organization. Additionally, configure your developer settings, which involve adding contact information and setting up tax details.

Step 3: Create a New Application

Inside the Google Play Console dashboard, click on "Create Application" to initiate the process of adding a new app to the store. Fill in the basic information for your app, such as the default language, title, and description. You'll then need to upload your app's APK (Android Package) or create an App Bundle.

Next, complete the store listing by adding details like screenshots, graphics, and a promotional video. Set the pricing and distribution preferences, choosing whether your app will be free or paid and selecting the countries where you want it to be available.

Step 4: Set Up In-App Products and Subscriptions (if applicable)

If your app includes in-app purchases or subscriptions, navigate to the "Monetize" section and configure the relevant details.

Step 5: Test Your App

Before releasing your app to the public, it's advisable to test it thoroughly. Google Play Console allows you to set up closed alpha or beta testing, allowing a limited group of users to try out your app and provide feedback.

Step 6: Publish Your App

Once you've completed all the necessary steps and are satisfied with your app's listing, submit it for review. Google will assess your app to ensure it complies with their policies. Once approved, your app will be published on the Google Play Store and made available to users.

Step 7: Manage Your App

After your app is live, use the Google Play Console to monitor its performance. You can track user statistics, reviews, and other relevant metrics. Regularly update your app to address any bugs, introduce new features, and enhance the overall user experience.

Content Rating and Policies in Play Console

When you publish an app on the Google Play Store, you are required to set up content ratings and adhere to certain policies to ensure that your app aligns with Google's guidelines. This is crucial for maintaining a safe and enjoyable experience for users. Here's an overview of content rating and policies in the Google Play Console:

Content Rating:

1. Content Rating Questionnaire:

Google Play uses a content rating questionnaire to assess the maturity level of your app's content. This helps users make informed decisions about the appropriateness of your app for different audiences.

2. Categories for Rating:

The questionnaire covers various categories, including violence, sexual content, substance abuse, and more. You'll be asked to provide information about the presence and intensity of content in each category.

3. Content Descriptors:

Based on your responses, Google Play will suggest content descriptors that best describe your app. These descriptors provide additional information about the content of your app to users.

4. Multiple Ratings:

If your app includes different types of content, you may need to go through the questionnaire multiple times to accurately represent the overall content of your app.

5. Impact on App Visibility:

The content rating assigned to your app can impact its visibility on the Play Store. Apps with certain content ratings may have restricted visibility in certain regions or age groups.

Policies:

1. Google Play Developer Program Policies:

Developers must comply with the Google Play Developer Program Policies. These policies cover various aspects, including prohibited content, intellectual property, privacy, and more.

2. Prohibited Content:

Google Play prohibits the distribution of certain types of content, such as illegal activities, hate speech, and sexually explicit material.

3. Sensitive Content:

Developers are required to be mindful of sensitive content and provide appropriate warnings or age restrictions. For example, apps containing mature or adult content must be properly rated.

4. Privacy Policy:

If your app collects personal or sensitive information, you are required to have a privacy policy in place. The privacy policy should be accessible to users and provide details about the information collected and how it is used.

5. App Review Process:

Google Play conducts a review of apps to ensure compliance with these policies. Failure to adhere to the policies may result in rejection or removal of the app from the Play Store.

6. Updates and Enforcement:

Developers are responsible for keeping their apps in compliance with policies, and updates may be subject to review. Google Play enforces policies to maintain a secure and positive user experience.

Ensuring that your app meets content rating requirements and complies with policies is essential for a successful and sustainable presence on the Google Play Store.

CHAPTER 10

ANDROID HANDS-ON (EXAMPLES)

The Android Studio examples presented above serve as invaluable and practical learning exercises tailored for beginners venturing into the realm of Android development. Each example is meticulously designed to impart foundational skills, providing learners with a hands-on experience that is crucial for building a solid understanding of Android app development.

Learners gain hands-on experience by building and running actual Android apps. This practical experience is invaluable for solidifying theoretical knowledge. The examples reinforce fundamental concepts in Android development, including UI design, event handling, and data management.

Learners can adapt these examples as starting points for their own projects, gradually building more complex applications by combining and extending the concepts learned. The examples mirror real-world scenarios, providing learners with skills applicable to a wide range of Android app development projects.

By working through these examples, learners can build a strong foundation in Android development, preparing them for more advanced topics and projects in the Android ecosystem.

Overall, these examples provide a holistic and incremental approach to Android development, progressively building from foundational concepts to more sophisticated topics. The hands-on nature of these exercises ensures that learners not only grasp theoretical concepts but also develop practical skills that can be directly applied to real-world projects. The adaptability of these examples allows beginners to use them as a springboard for their own creative endeavors, fostering a sense of confidence and self-sufficiency in Android app development. As learners progress through these exercises, they lay the groundwork for a successful journey into the multifaceted and ever-evolving field of Android development.

Hands-On 1: Hello World

XML (activity_main.xml):

```xml
<!-- res/layout/activity_main.xml -->
<?xml version="1.0" encoding="utf-8"?>
<RelativeLayout xmlns:android="http://schemas.android.com/apk/res/android"
    xmlns:tools="http://schemas.android.com/tools"
    android:layout_width="match_parent"
    android:layout_height="match_parent"
    tools:context=".MainActivity">

    <TextView
        android:id="@+id/helloTextView"
        android:layout_width="wrap_content"
        android:layout_height="wrap_content"
        android:text="Hello World!"
        android:layout_centerInParent="true"/>
```

```
</RelativeLayout>
```

Java (MainActivity.java):

```java
// java/com.example.helloworldapp/MainActivity.java
package com.example.helloworldapp;

import androidx.appcompat.app.AppCompatActivity;
import android.os.Bundle;

public class MainActivity extends AppCompatActivity {
    @Override
    protected void onCreate(Bundle savedInstanceState) {
        super.onCreate(savedInstanceState);
        setContentView(R.layout.activity_main);
    }
}
```

Hands-On 2: Quiz App

Building a quiz app involves creating questions, handling user input, and providing feedback on their answers. Below is a simple example of a quiz app in Android using Java. This example assumes a multiple-choice quiz with a fixed set of questions.

Create Question class (Question.java):

```java
// Question.java
public class Question {
    private String questionText;
    private String[] options;
    private int correctOptionIndex;

    public Question(String questionText, String[] options, int correctOptionIndex) {
        this.questionText = questionText;
        this.options = options;
        this.correctOptionIndex = correctOptionIndex;
    }

    public String getQuestionText() {
        return questionText;
    }

    public String[] getOptions() {
        return options;
    }
```

```java
    public int getCorrectOptionIndex() {
        return correctOptionIndex;
    }
}
```

Create QuizActivity class (QuizActivity.java):

```java
// QuizActivity.java
public class QuizActivity extends AppCompatActivity {

    private TextView questionTextView;
    private RadioGroup optionsRadioGroup;

    private List<Question> questions;
    private int currentQuestionIndex = 0;

    @Override
    protected void onCreate(Bundle savedInstanceState) {
        super.onCreate(savedInstanceState);
        setContentView(R.layout.activity_quiz);

        questionTextView = findViewById(R.id.questionTextView);
        optionsRadioGroup = findViewById(R.id.optionsRadioGroup);

        // Initialize the list of questions
        questions = initializeQuestions();

        // Display the first question
        displayQuestion();

        // Set up a button to submit the answer
        Button submitButton = findViewById(R.id.submitButton);
        submitButton.setOnClickListener(new View.OnClickListener() {
            @Override
            public void onClick(View v) {
                checkAnswer();
            }
        });
    }

    private List<Question> initializeQuestions() {
        // Create and return a list of quiz questions
        List<Question> questions = new ArrayList<>();
        questions.add(new Question("What is the capital of France?", new
String[]{"Berlin", "Paris", "Madrid", "Rome"}, 1));
        questions.add(new Question("Which planet is known as the Red
Planet?", new String[]{"Earth", "Mars", "Jupiter", "Venus"}, 1));
        // Add more questions here...
        return questions;
    }
```

```java
    private void displayQuestion() {
        // Display the current question
        Question currentQuestion = questions.get(currentQuestionIndex);
        questionTextView.setText(currentQuestion.getQuestionText());

        // Clear previous options
        optionsRadioGroup.removeAllViews();

        // Add radio buttons for each option
        for (int i = 0; i < currentQuestion.getOptions().length; i++) {
            RadioButton radioButton = new RadioButton(this);
            radioButton.setText(currentQuestion.getOptions()[i]);
            optionsRadioGroup.addView(radioButton);
        }
    }


    private void checkAnswer() {
        // Check the selected option against the correct answer
        int selectedOptionIndex =
optionsRadioGroup.indexOfChild(findViewById(optionsRadioGroup.getCheckedRad
ioButtonId()));
        Question currentQuestion = questions.get(currentQuestionIndex);

        if (selectedOptionIndex == currentQuestion.getCorrectOptionIndex())
{
            // Correct answer
            Toast.makeText(this, "Correct!", Toast.LENGTH_SHORT).show();
        } else {
            // Incorrect answer
            Toast.makeText(this, "Incorrect. The correct answer is " +
currentQuestion.getOptions()[currentQuestion.getCorrectOptionIndex()],
Toast.LENGTH_LONG).show();
        }

        // Move to the next question
        currentQuestionIndex++;

        if (currentQuestionIndex < questions.size()) {
            // Display the next question
            displayQuestion();
        } else {
            // End of the quiz
            Toast.makeText(this, "Quiz completed!",
Toast.LENGTH_SHORT).show();
        }
    }
}
```

Create activity_quiz.xml layout:

```xml
<!-- res/layout/activity_quiz.xml -->
<?xml version="1.0" encoding="utf-8"?>
<RelativeLayout xmlns:android="http://schemas.android.com/apk/res/android"
    xmlns:tools="http://schemas.android.com/tools"
    android:layout_width="match_parent"
    android:layout_height="match_parent"
    tools:context=".QuizActivity">

    <TextView
        android:id="@+id/questionTextView"
        android:layout_width="match_parent"
        android:layout_height="wrap_content"
        android:text="Question Text"
        android:layout_margin="16dp"
        android:textSize="18sp"/>

    <RadioGroup
        android:id="@+id/optionsRadioGroup"
        android:layout_width="match_parent"
        android:layout_height="wrap_content"
        android:layout_below="@id/questionTextView"
        android:layout_margin="16dp">

        <!-- Options will be added dynamically in code -->

    </RadioGroup>

    <Button
        android:id="@+id/submitButton"
        android:layout_width="wrap_content"
        android:layout_height="wrap_content"
        android:text="Submit"
        android:layout_below="@id/optionsRadioGroup"
        android:layout_centerHorizontal="true"
        android:layout_marginTop="16dp"/>
</RelativeLayout>
```

This code provides a simple framework for a quiz app with multiple-choice questions. You can customize and extend it based on your specific requirements, such as adding more questions, improving the user interface, or implementing features like scoring and timers.

Hands-On 3: Flashlight/Torchlight App

Creating a flashlight app in Android involves accessing the device's camera flash and controlling it to turn on and off. Below is a basic example of a flashlight app using Android Studio and Java. Note that using the camera flash requires the CAMERA permission.

Create FlashlightActivity class:

```java
// FlashlightActivity.java
public class FlashlightActivity extends AppCompatActivity {

    private CameraManager cameraManager;
    private String cameraId;
    private boolean isFlashlightOn = false;

    @Override
    protected void onCreate(Bundle savedInstanceState) {
        super.onCreate(savedInstanceState);
        setContentView(R.layout.activity_flashlight);

        // Check if the device has a flash
        if
(!getPackageManager().hasSystemFeature(PackageManager.FEATURE_CAMERA_FLASH)
) {
            Toast.makeText(this, "This device doesn't have a flash",
Toast.LENGTH_SHORT).show();
            finish();
            return;
        }

        // Initialize CameraManager
        cameraManager = (CameraManager)
getSystemService(Context.CAMERA_SERVICE);
        try {
            cameraId = cameraManager.getCameraIdList()[0];
        } catch (CameraAccessException e) {
            e.printStackTrace();
        }

        // Set up a button to toggle the flashlight
        Button toggleButton = findViewById(R.id.toggleButton);
        toggleButton.setOnClickListener(new View.OnClickListener() {
            @Override
            public void onClick(View v) {
                toggleFlashlight();
            }
        });
    }
```

```java
    private void toggleFlashlight() {
        try {
            if (isFlashlightOn) {
                // Turn off the flashlight
                cameraManager.setTorchMode(cameraId, false);
                isFlashlightOn = false;
            } else {
                // Turn on the flashlight
                cameraManager.setTorchMode(cameraId, true);
                isFlashlightOn = true;
            }
        } catch (CameraAccessException e) {
            e.printStackTrace();
        }
    }

    @Override
    protected void onStop() {
        super.onStop();
        // Turn off the flashlight when the app is stopped
        if (isFlashlightOn) {
            toggleFlashlight();
        }
    }
}
```

Create activity_flashlight.xml layout:

```xml
<!-- res/layout/activity_flashlight.xml -->
<?xml version="1.0" encoding="utf-8"?>
<RelativeLayout xmlns:android="http://schemas.android.com/apk/res/android"
    android:layout_width="match_parent"
    android:layout_height="match_parent"
    android:padding="16dp">

    <Button
        android:id="@+id/toggleButton"
        android:layout_width="wrap_content"
        android:layout_height="wrap_content"
        android:text="Toggle Flashlight"
        android:layout_centerInParent="true"/>
</RelativeLayout>
```

Add Permissions to Manifest:

- Open the AndroidManifest.xml file and add the following permissions:

```xml
<uses-permission android:name="android.permission.CAMERA" />
```

Hands-On 4: Stopwatch App

Creating a stopwatch app involves implementing a timer that can start, stop, and reset. Below is a simple example of a stopwatch app using Android Studio and Java.

Create StopwatchActivity class:

```java
// StopwatchActivity.java
public class StopwatchActivity extends AppCompatActivity {

    private Chronometer chronometer;
    private Button startButton, stopButton, resetButton;
    private boolean isRunning = false;

    @Override
    protected void onCreate(Bundle savedInstanceState) {
        super.onCreate(savedInstanceState);
        setContentView(R.layout.activity_stopwatch);

        chronometer = findViewById(R.id.chronometer);
        startButton = findViewById(R.id.startButton);
        stopButton = findViewById(R.id.stopButton);
        resetButton = findViewById(R.id.resetButton);

        startButton.setOnClickListener(new View.OnClickListener() {
            @Override
            public void onClick(View v) {
                startStopwatch();
            }
        });

        stopButton.setOnClickListener(new View.OnClickListener() {
            @Override
            public void onClick(View v) {
                stopStopwatch();
            }
        });

        resetButton.setOnClickListener(new View.OnClickListener() {
            @Override
            public void onClick(View v) {
                resetStopwatch();
            }
        });
    }

    private void startStopwatch() {
        if (!isRunning) {
```

```java
            chronometer.setBase(SystemClock.elapsedRealtime() -
chronometer.getBase());
            chronometer.start();
            isRunning = true;
        }
    }

    private void stopStopwatch() {
        if (isRunning) {
            chronometer.stop();
            isRunning = false;
        }
    }

    private void resetStopwatch() {
        chronometer.setBase(SystemClock.elapsedRealtime());
        if (isRunning) {
            chronometer.start();
        } else {
            chronometer.stop();
        }
    }
}
```

Create activity_stopwatch.xml layout:

```xml
<!-- res/layout/activity_stopwatch.xml -->
<?xml version="1.0" encoding="utf-8"?>
<RelativeLayout xmlns:android="http://schemas.android.com/apk/res/android"
    android:layout_width="match_parent"
    android:layout_height="match_parent"
    android:padding="16dp">

    <Chronometer
        android:id="@+id/chronometer"
        android:layout_width="wrap_content"
        android:layout_height="wrap_content"
        android:textSize="24sp"
        android:layout_centerHorizontal="true"/>

    <Button
        android:id="@+id/startButton"
        android:layout_width="wrap_content"
        android:layout_height="wrap_content"
        android:text="Start"
        android:layout_below="@id/chronometer"
        android:layout_marginTop="16dp"
        android:layout_centerHorizontal="true"/>
```

```xml
    <Button
        android:id="@+id/stopButton"
        android:layout_width="wrap_content"
        android:layout_height="wrap_content"
        android:text="Stop"
        android:layout_below="@id/startButton"
        android:layout_marginTop="16dp"
        android:layout_centerHorizontal="true"/>

    <Button
        android:id="@+id/resetButton"
        android:layout_width="wrap_content"
        android:layout_height="wrap_content"
        android:text="Reset"
        android:layout_below="@id/stopButton"
        android:layout_marginTop="16dp"
        android:layout_centerHorizontal="true"/>
</RelativeLayout>
```

Hands-On 5: Simple Notes App

Creating a simple notes app involves creating a user interface to input and display notes, as well as storing and retrieving them. Below is a basic example of a simple notes app using Android Studio and Java with a simple data storage approach.

Create Note class:

```java
// Note.java
public class Note {
    private String title;
    private String content;

    public Note(String title, String content) {
        this.title = title;
        this.content = content;
    }

    public String getTitle() {
        return title;
    }

    public String getContent() {
        return content;
    }
}
```

Create NotesActivity class:

```java
// NotesActivity.java
public class NotesActivity extends AppCompatActivity {

    private EditText titleEditText, contentEditText;
    private Button saveButton, viewButton;
    private List<Note> notesList;

    @Override
    protected void onCreate(Bundle savedInstanceState) {
        super.onCreate(savedInstanceState);
        setContentView(R.layout.activity_notes);

        titleEditText = findViewById(R.id.titleEditText);
        contentEditText = findViewById(R.id.contentEditText);
        saveButton = findViewById(R.id.saveButton);
        viewButton = findViewById(R.id.viewButton);

        notesList = new ArrayList<>();

        saveButton.setOnClickListener(new View.OnClickListener() {
            @Override
            public void onClick(View v) {
                saveNote();
            }
        });

        viewButton.setOnClickListener(new View.OnClickListener() {
            @Override
            public void onClick(View v) {
                viewNotes();
            }
        });
    }

    private void saveNote() {
        String title = titleEditText.getText().toString().trim();
        String content = contentEditText.getText().toString().trim();

        if (!TextUtils.isEmpty(title) && !TextUtils.isEmpty(content)) {
            Note newNote = new Note(title, content);
            notesList.add(newNote);

            Toast.makeText(this, "Note saved successfully",
Toast.LENGTH_SHORT).show();

            // Clear input fields
            titleEditText.getText().clear();
            contentEditText.getText().clear();
        } else {
```

```java
            Toast.makeText(this, "Please enter both title and content",
Toast.LENGTH_SHORT).show();
        }
    }

    private void viewNotes() {
        Intent intent = new Intent(this, ViewNotesActivity.class);
        intent.putExtra("notesList", (Serializable) notesList);
        startActivity(intent);
    }
}
```

Create ViewNotesActivity class:

```java
// ViewNotesActivity.java
public class ViewNotesActivity extends AppCompatActivity {

    private ListView notesListView;

    @Override
    protected void onCreate(Bundle savedInstanceState) {
        super.onCreate(savedInstanceState);
        setContentView(R.layout.activity_view_notes);

        notesListView = findViewById(R.id.notesListView);

        // Retrieve notes list from the intent
        Intent intent = getIntent();
        List<Note> notesList = (List<Note>)
intent.getSerializableExtra("notesList");

        if (notesList != null) {
            // Display notes using a simple ArrayAdapter
            ArrayAdapter<Note> adapter = new ArrayAdapter<>(this,
android.R.layout.simple_list_item_1, notesList);
            notesListView.setAdapter(adapter);
        }
    }
}
```

Create activity_notes.xml layout:

```xml
<!-- res/layout/activity_notes.xml -->
<?xml version="1.0" encoding="utf-8"?>
<RelativeLayout xmlns:android="http://schemas.android.com/apk/res/android"
    android:layout_width="match_parent"
    android:layout_height="match_parent"
    android:padding="16dp">
```

```xml
    <EditText
        android:id="@+id/titleEditText"
        android:layout_width="match_parent"
        android:layout_height="wrap_content"
        android:hint="Title"
        android:layout_marginBottom="8dp"/>

    <EditText
        android:id="@+id/contentEditText"
        android:layout_width="match_parent"
        android:layout_height="wrap_content"
        android:hint="Content"
        android:layout_below="@id/titleEditText"
        android:layout_marginTop="8dp"
        android:layout_marginBottom="16dp"/>

    <Button
        android:id="@+id/saveButton"
        android:layout_width="wrap_content"
        android:layout_height="wrap_content"
        android:text="Save"
        android:layout_below="@id/contentEditText"
        android:layout_marginTop="16dp"
        android:layout_marginEnd="8dp"/>

    <Button
        android:id="@+id/viewButton"
        android:layout_width="wrap_content"
        android:layout_height="wrap_content"
        android:text="View Notes"
        android:layout_below="@id/contentEditText"
        android:layout_marginTop="16dp"
        android:layout_toEndOf="@id/saveButton"
        android:layout_marginStart="8dp"/>
</RelativeLayout>
```

Create activity_view_notes.xml layout:

```xml
<!-- res/layout/activity_view_notes.xml -->
<?xml version="1.0" encoding="utf-8"?>
<RelativeLayout xmlns:android="http://schemas.android.com/apk/res/android"
    android:layout_width="match_parent"
    android:layout_height="match_parent"
    android:padding="16dp">

    <ListView
        android:id="@+id/notesListView"
```

```xml
            android:layout_width="match_parent"
            android:layout_height="match_parent"/>
</RelativeLayout>
```

Add Activities to Manifest:

- Open the AndroidManifest.xml file and add the following entries:

```xml
<activity android:name=".NotesActivity" />
<activity android:name=".ViewNotesActivity" />
```

Now, you have a basic notes app that allows users to input notes with titles and content. The notes are stored in a list and can be viewed in another activity. This example provides a starting point, and you can further enhance the app by adding features such as persistent storage, editing and deleting notes, and more.

Hands-On 6: QR Code Reader

To create a QR code reader app in Android, you can use the ZXing (pronounced "zebra crossing") library. ZXing is a widely-used library for reading and generating QR codes. Below is an example of a simple QR code reader app using ZXing.

Add ZXing Library Dependency:

- Open the build.gradle (Module: app) file.
- Add the ZXing library dependency:

```
implementation 'com.google.zxing:core:3.4.0'
implementation 'com.journeyapps:zxing-android-embedded:3.6.0'
```

Request Camera Permission:

- Open the AndroidManifest.xml file.
- Add the following permission:

```xml
<uses-permission android:name="android.permission.CAMERA" />
```

Create QRCodeReaderActivity class:

```java
// QRCodeReaderActivity.java
public class QRCodeReaderActivity extends AppCompatActivity implements
ZXingScannerView.ResultHandler {

    private ZXingScannerView scannerView;

    @Override
    protected void onCreate(Bundle savedInstanceState) {
        super.onCreate(savedInstanceState);
        scannerView = new ZXingScannerView(this);
```

```java
        setContentView(scannerView);
    }

    @Override
    public void onResume() {
        super.onResume();
        // Start the camera when the activity is resumed
        scannerView.setResultHandler(this);
        scannerView.startCamera();
    }

    @Override
    public void onPause() {
        super.onPause();
        // Stop the camera when the activity is paused
        scannerView.stopCamera();
    }

    @Override
    public void handleResult(Result result) {
        // Handle the result from the QR code scan
        String scannedText = result.getText();

        // You can use the scanned text as needed (e.g., display it, pass
it to another activity, etc.)
        Toast.makeText(this, "Scanned: " + scannedText,
Toast.LENGTH_SHORT).show();

        // Resume scanning for more codes
        scannerView.resumeCameraPreview(this);
    }
}
```

Add the QRCodeReaderActivity to the Manifest:

Open the AndroidManifest.xml file and add the following entry:

```xml
<activity android:name=".QRCodeReaderActivity">
    <intent-filter>
        <action android:name="android.intent.action.MAIN" />
        <category android:name="android.intent.category.LAUNCHER" />
    </intent-filter>
</activity>
```

Now, you have a simple QR code reader app using the ZXing library. When the app is launched, the camera will start, and you can scan QR codes by pointing the camera at them. The scanned text will be displayed in a Toast message in this example.

Hands-On 7: Simple Alarm

Creating an alarm app involves setting up alarms, handling notifications, and allowing users to manage their alarms. Below is a basic example of an alarm app using Android Studio and Java.

Create AlarmActivity class:

```java
// AlarmActivity.java
public class AlarmActivity extends AppCompatActivity {

    private AlarmManager alarmManager;
    private PendingIntent alarmIntent;
    private EditText editTextTime;

    @Override
    protected void onCreate(Bundle savedInstanceState) {
        super.onCreate(savedInstanceState);
        setContentView(R.layout.activity_alarm);

        editTextTime = findViewById(R.id.editTextTime);

        alarmManager = (AlarmManager) getSystemService(ALARM_SERVICE);

        Intent intent = new Intent(this, AlarmReceiver.class);
        alarmIntent = PendingIntent.getBroadcast(this, 0, intent, 0);

        Button setAlarmButton = findViewById(R.id.setAlarmButton);
        setAlarmButton.setOnClickListener(new View.OnClickListener() {
            @Override
            public void onClick(View v) {
                setAlarm();
            }
        });

        Button cancelAlarmButton = findViewById(R.id.cancelAlarmButton);
        cancelAlarmButton.setOnClickListener(new View.OnClickListener() {
            @Override
            public void onClick(View v) {
                cancelAlarm();
            }
        });
    }

    private void setAlarm() {
        String timeString = editTextTime.getText().toString().trim();

        if (!TextUtils.isEmpty(timeString)) {
            int timeInMillis = Integer.parseInt(timeString) * 1000; //
Convert seconds to milliseconds
```

```java
        // Set the alarm
        alarmManager.set(AlarmManager.ELAPSED_REALTIME_WAKEUP,
                SystemClock.elapsedRealtime() + timeInMillis,
                alarmIntent);

        Toast.makeText(this, "Alarm set for " + timeString + " seconds",
Toast.LENGTH_SHORT).show();
        } else {
            Toast.makeText(this,    "Please    enter    a    valid    time",
Toast.LENGTH_SHORT).show();
        }
    }

    private void cancelAlarm() {
        // Cancel the alarm
        alarmManager.cancel(alarmIntent);
        Toast.makeText(this, "Alarm canceled", Toast.LENGTH_SHORT).show();
    }
}
```

Create AlarmReceiver class:

```java
// AlarmReceiver.java
public class AlarmReceiver extends BroadcastReceiver {

    @Override
    public void onReceive(Context context, Intent intent) {
        // Handle the alarm event, e.g., show a notification
        showNotification(context, "Alarm", "Time's up!");
    }

    private void showNotification(Context context, String title, String
message) {
        NotificationManager notificationManager = (NotificationManager)
context.getSystemService(Context.NOTIFICATION_SERVICE);

        // Create a notification channel for devices running Android 8.0 (API
level 26) and higher
        if (Build.VERSION.SDK_INT >= Build.VERSION_CODES.O) {
            NotificationChannel channel = new NotificationChannel("default",
"Channel Name",
                    NotificationManager.IMPORTANCE_DEFAULT);
            notificationManager.createNotificationChannel(channel);
        }

        NotificationCompat.Builder builder = new
NotificationCompat.Builder(context, "default")
```

```java
                .setSmallIcon(R.drawable.ic_launcher_foreground)
                .setContentTitle(title)
                .setContentText(message)
                .setPriority(NotificationCompat.PRIORITY_DEFAULT);

        notificationManager.notify(1, builder.build());
    }
}
```

Create activity_alarm.xml layout:

```xml
<!-- res/layout/activity_alarm.xml -->
<?xml version="1.0" encoding="utf-8"?>
<RelativeLayout xmlns:android="http://schemas.android.com/apk/res/android"
    android:layout_width="match_parent"
    android:layout_height="match_parent"
    android:padding="16dp">

    <EditText
        android:id="@+id/editTextTime"
        android:layout_width="match_parent"
        android:layout_height="wrap_content"
        android:hint="Enter time in seconds"
        android:inputType="number"
        android:layout_marginBottom="16dp"/>

    <Button
        android:id="@+id/setAlarmButton"
        android:layout_width="wrap_content"
        android:layout_height="wrap_content"
        android:text="Set Alarm"
        android:layout_below="@id/editTextTime"
        android:layout_marginTop="16dp"/>

    <Button
        android:id="@+id/cancelAlarmButton"
        android:layout_width="wrap_content"
        android:layout_height="wrap_content"
        android:text="Cancel Alarm"
        android:layout_below="@id/setAlarmButton"
        android:layout_marginTop="16dp"/>
</RelativeLayout>
```

Add AlarmActivity and AlarmReceiver to the Manifest:

Open the AndroidManifest.xml file and add the following entries:

```xml
<activity android:name=".AlarmActivity">
```

```xml
    <intent-filter>
        <action android:name="android.intent.action.MAIN" />
        <category android:name="android.intent.category.LAUNCHER" />
    </intent-filter>
</activity>

<receiver android:name=".AlarmReceiver" />
```

Now, you have a basic alarm app that allows users to set alarms and cancel them. When the alarm triggers, a notification will be shown. Customize the code as needed for your specific requirements.

Hands-On 8: Contacts App

Creating a contacts app involves managing a list of contacts, allowing users to add, view, edit, and delete contacts. Below is a basic example of a contacts app using Android Studio and Java.

Create Contact class:

```java
// Contact.java
public class Contact implements Serializable {
    private String name;
    private String phone;

    public Contact(String name, String phone) {
        this.name = name;
        this.phone = phone;
    }

    public String getName() {
        return name;
    }

    public String getPhone() {
        return phone;
    }

    @Override
    public String toString() {
        return name + ": " + phone;
    }
}
```

Create ContactsActivity class:

```java
// ContactsActivity.java
public class ContactsActivity extends AppCompatActivity {

    private List<Contact> contactsList;
```

```java
    private ArrayAdapter<Contact> adapter;

    @Override
    protected void onCreate(Bundle savedInstanceState) {
        super.onCreate(savedInstanceState);
        setContentView(R.layout.activity_contacts);

        contactsList = new ArrayList<>();
        adapter = new ArrayAdapter<>(this,
android.R.layout.simple_list_item_1, contactsList);

        ListView contactsListView = findViewById(R.id.contactsListView);
        contactsListView.setAdapter(adapter);

        contactsListView.setOnItemClickListener(new
AdapterView.OnItemClickListener() {
            @Override
            public void onItemClick(AdapterView<?> parent, View view, int
position, long id) {
                editContact(position);
            }
        });

        Button addContactButton = findViewById(R.id.addContactButton);
        addContactButton.setOnClickListener(new View.OnClickListener() {
            @Override
            public void onClick(View v) {
                addContact();
            }
        });

        Button deleteAllButton = findViewById(R.id.deleteAllButton);
        deleteAllButton.setOnClickListener(new View.OnClickListener() {
            @Override
            public void onClick(View v) {
                deleteAllContacts();
            }
        });
    }

    private void addContact() {
        // Launch AddContactActivity to add a new contact
        Intent intent = new Intent(this, AddContactActivity.class);
        startActivityForResult(intent, 1);
    }

    private void editContact(int position) {
        // Launch EditContactActivity to edit an existing contact
        Intent intent = new Intent(this, EditContactActivity.class);
```

```java
            intent.putExtra("contact", contactsList.get(position));
            intent.putExtra("position", position);
            startActivityForResult(intent, 2);
    }

    private void deleteAllContacts() {
        // Delete all contacts
        contactsList.clear();
        adapter.notifyDataSetChanged();
        Toast.makeText(this, "All contacts deleted",
Toast.LENGTH_SHORT).show();
    }

    @Override
    protected void onActivityResult(int requestCode, int resultCode, Intent
data) {
        super.onActivityResult(requestCode, resultCode, data);

        if (resultCode == RESULT_OK) {
            if (requestCode == 1) {
                // Add a new contact
                Contact newContact = (Contact)
data.getSerializableExtra("contact");
                contactsList.add(newContact);
                adapter.notifyDataSetChanged();
                Toast.makeText(this, "Contact added",
Toast.LENGTH_SHORT).show();
            } else if (requestCode == 2) {
                // Edit an existing contact
                int position = data.getIntExtra("position", -1);
                Contact editedContact = (Contact)
data.getSerializableExtra("contact");

                if (position != -1) {
                    contactsList.set(position, editedContact);
                    adapter.notifyDataSetChanged();
                    Toast.makeText(this, "Contact edited",
Toast.LENGTH_SHORT).show();
                }
            }
        }
    }
}
```

Create AddContactActivity class:

```java
// AddContactActivity.java
public class AddContactActivity extends AppCompatActivity {
```

```java
    private EditText nameEditText, phoneEditText;

    @Override
    protected void onCreate(Bundle savedInstanceState) {
        super.onCreate(savedInstanceState);
        setContentView(R.layout.activity_add_contact);

        nameEditText = findViewById(R.id.nameEditText);
        phoneEditText = findViewById(R.id.phoneEditText);

        Button saveButton = findViewById(R.id.saveButton);
        saveButton.setOnClickListener(new View.OnClickListener() {
            @Override
            public void onClick(View v) {
                saveContact();
            }
        });
    }

    private void saveContact() {
        String name = nameEditText.getText().toString().trim();
        String phone = phoneEditText.getText().toString().trim();

        if (!TextUtils.isEmpty(name) && !TextUtils.isEmpty(phone)) {
            Contact newContact = new Contact(name, phone);

            Intent resultIntent = new Intent();
            resultIntent.putExtra("contact", newContact);
            setResult(RESULT_OK, resultIntent);
            finish();
        } else {
            Toast.makeText(this, "Please enter both name and phone number",
Toast.LENGTH_SHORT).show();
        }
    }
}
```

Create EditContactActivity class:

```java
// EditContactActivity.java
public class EditContactActivity extends AppCompatActivity {

    private EditText nameEditText, phoneEditText;
    private Contact originalContact;
    private int position;

    @Override
```

```java
    protected void onCreate(Bundle savedInstanceState) {
        super.onCreate(savedInstanceState);
        setContentView(R.layout.activity_edit_contact);

        nameEditText = findViewById(R.id.nameEditText);
        phoneEditText = findViewById(R.id.phoneEditText);

        // Retrieve the original contact and position from the intent
        originalContact = (Contact)
getIntent().getSerializableExtra("contact");
        position = getIntent().getIntExtra("position", -1);

        if (originalContact != null) {
            nameEditText.setText(originalContact.getName());
            phoneEditText.setText(originalContact.getPhone());
        }

        Button saveButton = findViewById(R.id.saveButton);
        saveButton.setOnClickListener(new View.OnClickListener() {
            @Override
            public void onClick(View v) {
                saveContact();
            }
        });
    }

    private void saveContact() {
        String name = nameEditText.getText().toString().trim();
        String phone = phoneEditText.getText().toString().trim();

        if (!TextUtils.isEmpty(name) && !TextUtils.isEmpty(phone)) {
            Contact editedContact = new Contact(name, phone);

            Intent resultIntent = new Intent();
            resultIntent.putExtra("contact", editedContact);
            resultIntent.putExtra("position", position);
            setResult(RESULT_OK, resultIntent);
            finish();
        } else {
            Toast.makeText(this, "Please enter both name and phone number",
Toast.LENGTH_SHORT).show();
        }
    }
}
```

Create activity_contacts.xml layout:

```xml
<!-- res/layout/activity_contacts.xml -->
```

```xml
<?xml version="1.0" encoding="utf-8"?>
<RelativeLayout xmlns:android="http://schemas.android.com/apk/res/android"
    android:layout_width="match_parent"
    android:layout_height="match_parent"
    android:padding="16dp">

    <ListView
        android:id="@+id/contactsListView"
        android:layout_width="match_parent"
        android:layout_height="match_parent"
        android:layout_above="@+id/addContactButton"
        android:layout_marginBottom="16dp"/>

    <Button
        android:id="@+id/addContactButton"
        android:layout_width="wrap_content"
        android:layout_height="wrap_content"
        android:text="Add Contact"
        android:layout_alignParentBottom="true"
        android:layout_centerHorizontal="true"
        android:layout_marginBottom="16dp"/>

    <Button
        android:id="@+id/deleteAllButton"
        android:layout_width="wrap_content"
        android:layout_height="wrap_content"
        android:text="Delete All"
        android:layout_alignParentBottom="true"
        android:layout_alignParentEnd="true"
        android:layout_marginBottom="16dp"
        android:layout_marginEnd="16dp"/>
</RelativeLayout>
```

Create activity_add_contact.xml layout:

```xml
<!-- res/layout/activity_add_contact.xml -->
<?xml version="1.0" encoding="utf-8"?>
<RelativeLayout xmlns:android="http://schemas.android.com/apk/res/android"
    android:layout_width="match_parent"
    android:layout_height="match_parent"
    android:padding="16dp">

    <EditText
        android:id="@+id/nameEditText"
        android:layout_width="match_parent"
        android:layout_height="wrap_content"
        android:hint="Name"
        android:layout_marginBottom="8dp"/>
```

```xml
    <EditText
        android:id="@+id/phoneEditText"
        android:layout_width="match_parent"
        android:layout_height="wrap_content"
        android:inputType="phone"
        android:hint="Phone Number"
        android:layout_below="@id/nameEditText"
        android:layout_marginTop="8dp"
        android:layout_marginBottom="16dp"/>

    <Button
        android:id="@+id/saveButton"
        android:layout_width="wrap_content"
        android:layout_height="wrap_content"
        android:text="Save"
        android:layout_below="@id/phoneEditText"
        android:layout_marginTop="16dp"
        android:layout_marginEnd="8dp"/>
</RelativeLayout>
```

Create activity_edit_contact.xml layout:

```xml
<!-- res/layout/activity_edit_contact.xml -->
<?xml version="1.0" encoding="utf-8"?>
<RelativeLayout xmlns:android="http://schemas.android.com/apk/res/android"
    android:layout_width="match_parent"
    android:layout_height="match_parent"
    android:padding="16dp">

    <EditText
        android:id="@+id/nameEditText"
        android:layout_width="match_parent"
        android:layout_height="wrap_content"
        android:hint="Name"
        android:layout_marginBottom="8dp"/>

    <EditText
        android:id="@+id/phoneEditText"
        android:layout_width="match_parent"
        android:layout_height="wrap_content"
        android:inputType="phone"
        android:hint="Phone Number"
        android:layout_below="@id/nameEditText"
        android:layout_marginTop="8dp"
        android:layout_marginBottom="16dp"/>

    <Button
```

```
        android:id="@+id/saveButton"
        android:layout_width="wrap_content"
        android:layout_height="wrap_content"
        android:text="Save"
        android:layout_below="@id/phoneEditText"
        android:layout_marginTop="16dp"
        android:layout_marginEnd="8dp"/>
</RelativeLayout>
```

Add Activities to the Manifest:

Open the AndroidManifest.xml file and add the following entries:

```xml
<activity android:name=".ContactsActivity">
    <intent-filter>
        <action android:name="android.intent.action.MAIN" />
        <category android:name="android.intent.category.LAUNCHER" />
    </intent-filter>
</activity>

<activity android:name=".AddContactActivity" />
<activity android:name=".EditContactActivity" />
```

Now, you have a basic contacts app that allows users to add, view, edit, and delete contacts. Customize the code as needed for your specific requirements.

Hands-On 9: Simple Music Player

Creating a simple music player app involves playing audio files and providing basic controls for the user. Below is a basic example of a music player app using Android Studio and Java.

Create MusicPlayerActivity class:

```java
// MusicPlayerActivity.java
public class MusicPlayerActivity extends AppCompatActivity {

    private MediaPlayer mediaPlayer;
    private SeekBar seekBar;
    private TextView currentTimeTextView, totalTimeTextView;
    private Handler handler = new Handler();

    @Override
    protected void onCreate(Bundle savedInstanceState) {
        super.onCreate(savedInstanceState);
        setContentView(R.layout.activity_music_player);

        mediaPlayer = MediaPlayer.create(this, R.raw.sample_music);
        seekBar = findViewById(R.id.seekBar);
```

```java
        currentTimeTextView = findViewById(R.id.currentTimeTextView);
        totalTimeTextView = findViewById(R.id.totalTimeTextView);

        seekBar.setMax(mediaPlayer.getDuration());

        // Update seek bar and time text views
        updateSeekBar();

        // Start updating seek bar and time text views in a background
thread
        handler.postDelayed(updateTimeTask, 100);

        mediaPlayer.setOnCompletionListener(new
MediaPlayer.OnCompletionListener() {
            @Override
            public void onCompletion(MediaPlayer mp) {
                // Reset the player when playback is complete
                resetPlayer();
            }
        });

        ImageButton playPauseButton = findViewById(R.id.playPauseButton);
        playPauseButton.setOnClickListener(new View.OnClickListener() {
            @Override
            public void onClick(View v) {
                togglePlayPause();
            }
        });

        seekBar.setOnSeekBarChangeListener(new
SeekBar.OnSeekBarChangeListener() {
            @Override
            public void onProgressChanged(SeekBar seekBar, int progress,
boolean fromUser) {
                if (fromUser) {
                    // Seek to the specified position when the user drags
the seek bar
                    mediaPlayer.seekTo(progress);
                }
            }

            @Override
            public void onStartTrackingTouch(SeekBar seekBar) {
                // Pause the player when the user starts dragging the seek
bar
                mediaPlayer.pause();
            }

            @Override
```

```java
        public void onStopTrackingTouch(SeekBar seekBar) {
                // Resume playing when the user stops dragging the seek bar
                mediaPlayer.start();
            }
        });
    }

    private void togglePlayPause() {
        if (mediaPlayer.isPlaying()) {
            mediaPlayer.pause();
        } else {
            mediaPlayer.start();
        }
    }

    private void updateSeekBar() {
currentTimeTextView.setText(formatTime(mediaPlayer.getCurrentPosition()));
        totalTimeTextView.setText(formatTime(mediaPlayer.getDuration()));

        seekBar.setProgress(mediaPlayer.getCurrentPosition());
        handler.postDelayed(updateTimeTask, 100);
    }

    private Runnable updateTimeTask = new Runnable() {
        public void run() {
            updateSeekBar();
        }
    };

    private String formatTime(int milliseconds) {
        int seconds = (milliseconds / 1000) % 60;
        int minutes = (milliseconds / (1000 * 60)) % 60;
        return String.format(Locale.getDefault(), "%02d:%02d", minutes,
seconds);
    }

    private void resetPlayer() {
        mediaPlayer.seekTo(0);
        mediaPlayer.pause();
        updateSeekBar();
    }

    @Override
    protected void onDestroy() {
        super.onDestroy();
        // Release the media player when the activity is destroyed
        if (mediaPlayer != null) {
            mediaPlayer.release();
```

```java
            mediaPlayer = null;
        }
        // Remove callbacks to prevent memory leaks
        handler.removeCallbacks(updateTimeTask);
    }
}
```

Create activity_music_player.xml layout:

```xml
<!-- res/layout/activity_music_player.xml -->
<?xml version="1.0" encoding="utf-8"?>
<RelativeLayout xmlns:android="http://schemas.android.com/apk/res/android"
    android:layout_width="match_parent"
    android:layout_height="match_parent"
    android:padding="16dp">

    <SeekBar
        android:id="@+id/seekBar"
        android:layout_width="match_parent"
        android:layout_height="wrap_content"
        android:layout_centerVertical="true"
        android:layout_marginTop="16dp"
        android:layout_marginBottom="16dp"/>

    <TextView
        android:id="@+id/currentTimeTextView"
        android:layout_width="wrap_content"
        android:layout_height="wrap_content"
        android:layout_alignParentStart="true"
        android:layout_below="@id/seekBar"
        android:layout_marginTop="8dp"
        android:text="00:00"/>

    <TextView
        android:id="@+id/totalTimeTextView"
        android:layout_width="wrap_content"
        android:layout_height="wrap_content"
        android:layout_alignParentEnd="true"
        android:layout_below="@id/seekBar"
        android:layout_marginTop="8dp"
        android:text="00:00"/>

    <ImageButton
        android:id="@+id/playPauseButton"
        android:layout_width="wrap_content"
        android:layout_height="wrap_content"
        android:layout_centerHorizontal="true"
        android:layout_below="@id/currentTimeTextView"
```

```xml
        android:layout_marginTop="16dp"
        android:src="@android:drawable/ic_media_play"/>
</RelativeLayout>
```

Add MusicPlayerActivity to the Manifest:

Open the AndroidManifest.xml file and add the following entry:

```xml
<activity android:name=".MusicPlayerActivity">
    <intent-filter>
        <action android:name="android.intent.action.MAIN" />
        <category android:name="android.intent.category.LAUNCHER" />
    </intent-filter>
</activity>
```

Now, you have a basic music player app that plays a sample music file, displays the current and total time, and allows the user to play and pause the music. Customize the code and layout as needed for your specific requirements.

Hands-On 10: Firebase Login/Register using Email/Password

To create a simple login/register page using Firebase Authentication in Android, you can follow these steps. Firebase Authentication provides a secure and easy-to-use authentication system.

Step 1: Set up Firebase Project

Follow to procedure explained in chapter 6, to setup firebase successfully.

Step 2: Set up Firebase in Android Studio

- Open your Android Studio project.
- Add the Firebase SDK to your app by adding the following to the build.gradle file (Module: app):

```gradle
dependencies {
    // ...

    implementation 'com.google.firebase:firebase-auth:23.0.0' // Use the
latest version
}
```

- Sync your project with the updated Gradle files.

Step 3: Create the Login/Register Activity

- Create two XML layout files for login and registration screens:

activity_login.xml

```xml
<!-- res/layout/activity_login.xml -->
<?xml version="1.0" encoding="utf-8"?>
```

```xml
<RelativeLayout xmlns:android="http://schemas.android.com/apk/res/android"
    android:layout_width="match_parent"
    android:layout_height="match_parent"
    android:padding="16dp">

    <EditText
        android:id="@+id/emailEditText"
        android:layout_width="match_parent"
        android:layout_height="wrap_content"
        android:hint="Email"
        android:inputType="textEmailAddress"
        android:layout_marginBottom="16dp"/>

    <EditText
        android:id="@+id/passwordEditText"
        android:layout_width="match_parent"
        android:layout_height="wrap_content"
        android:hint="Password"
        android:inputType="textPassword"
        android:layout_below="@id/emailEditText"
        android:layout_marginTop="8dp"
        android:layout_marginBottom="16dp"/>

    <Button
        android:id="@+id/loginButton"
        android:layout_width="match_parent"
        android:layout_height="wrap_content"
        android:text="Login"
        android:layout_below="@id/passwordEditText"
        android:layout_marginTop="16dp"/>

    <TextView
        android:layout_width="wrap_content"
        android:layout_height="wrap_content"
        android:text="Don't have an account? "
        android:layout_below="@id/loginButton"
        android:layout_marginTop="16dp"/>

    <Button
        android:id="@+id/registerButton"
        android:layout_width="wrap_content"
        android:layout_height="wrap_content"
        android:text="Register"
        android:layout_toEndOf="@id/loginButton"
        android:layout_below="@id/loginButton"
        android:layout_marginTop="16dp"/>
</RelativeLayout>
```

activity_register.xml

```xml
<!-- res/layout/activity_register.xml -->
<?xml version="1.0" encoding="utf-8"?>
<RelativeLayout xmlns:android="http://schemas.android.com/apk/res/android"
    android:layout_width="match_parent"
    android:layout_height="match_parent"
    android:padding="16dp">

    <EditText
        android:id="@+id/registerEmailEditText"
        android:layout_width="match_parent"
        android:layout_height="wrap_content"
        android:hint="Email"
        android:inputType="textEmailAddress"
        android:layout_marginBottom="16dp"/>

    <EditText
        android:id="@+id/registerPasswordEditText"
        android:layout_width="match_parent"
        android:layout_height="wrap_content"
        android:hint="Password"
        android:inputType="textPassword"
        android:layout_below="@id/registerEmailEditText"
        android:layout_marginTop="8dp"
        android:layout_marginBottom="16dp"/>

    <Button
        android:id="@+id/registerButton"
        android:layout_width="match_parent"
        android:layout_height="wrap_content"
        android:text="Register"
        android:layout_below="@id/registerPasswordEditText"
        android:layout_marginTop="16dp"/>
</RelativeLayout>
```

Step 4: Implement Authentication Logic

- Create a new LoginActivity.java and RegisterActivity.java and implement the authentication logic.

LoginActivity.java

```java
// LoginActivity.java
public class LoginActivity extends AppCompatActivity {

    private EditText emailEditText, passwordEditText;
    private Button loginButton, registerButton;

    private FirebaseAuth firebaseAuth;
```

```java
    @Override
    protected void onCreate(Bundle savedInstanceState) {
        super.onCreate(savedInstanceState);
        setContentView(R.layout.activity_login);

        firebaseAuth = FirebaseAuth.getInstance();

        emailEditText = findViewById(R.id.emailEditText);
        passwordEditText = findViewById(R.id.passwordEditText);
        loginButton = findViewById(R.id.loginButton);
        registerButton = findViewById(R.id.registerButton);

        loginButton.setOnClickListener(new View.OnClickListener() {
            @Override
            public void onClick(View v) {
                loginUser();
            }
        });

        registerButton.setOnClickListener(new View.OnClickListener() {
            @Override
            public void onClick(View v) {
                startActivity(new Intent(LoginActivity.this,
RegisterActivity.class));
            }
        });
    }

    private void loginUser() {
        String email = emailEditText.getText().toString().trim();
        String password = passwordEditText.getText().toString().trim();

        if (TextUtils.isEmpty(email) || TextUtils.isEmpty(password)) {
            Toast.makeText(this, "Please fill in all fields",
Toast.LENGTH_SHORT).show();
            return;
        }

        firebaseAuth.signInWithEmailAndPassword(email, password)
                .addOnCompleteListener(this, new
OnCompleteListener<AuthResult>() {
                    @Override
                    public void onComplete(@NonNull Task<AuthResult> task)
{
                        if (task.isSuccessful()) {
                            startActivity(new Intent(LoginActivity.this,
HomeActivity.class));
                            finish();
```

```java
                } else {
                    Toast.makeText(LoginActivity.this, "Login
failed", Toast.LENGTH_SHORT).show();
                }
            }
        });
    }
}
```

RegisterActivity.java

```java
// RegisterActivity.java
public class RegisterActivity extends AppCompatActivity {

    private EditText registerEmailEditText, registerPasswordEditText;
    private Button registerButton;

    private FirebaseAuth firebaseAuth;

    @Override
    protected void onCreate(Bundle savedInstanceState) {
        super.onCreate(savedInstanceState);
        setContentView(R.layout.activity_register);

        firebaseAuth = FirebaseAuth.getInstance();

        registerEmailEditText = findViewById(R.id.registerEmailEditText);
        registerPasswordEditText =
findViewById(R.id.registerPasswordEditText);
        registerButton = findViewById(R.id.registerButton);

        registerButton.setOnClickListener(new View.OnClickListener() {
            @Override
            public void onClick(View v) {
                registerUser();
            }
        });
    }

    private void registerUser() {
        String email = registerEmailEditText.getText().toString().trim();
        String password =
registerPasswordEditText.getText().toString().trim();

        if (TextUtils.isEmpty(email) || TextUtils.isEmpty(password)) {
            Toast.makeText(this, "Please fill in all fields",
Toast.LENGTH_SHORT).show();
            return;
```

```java
        }

        firebaseAuth.createUserWithEmailAndPassword(email, password)
                .addOnCompleteListener(this, new
OnCompleteListener<AuthResult>() {
                    @Override
                    public void onComplete(@NonNull Task<AuthResult> task)
{
                        if (task.isSuccessful()) {
                            startActivity(new Intent(RegisterActivity.this,
HomeActivity.class));
                            finish();
                        } else {
                            Toast.makeText(RegisterActivity.this,
"Registration failed", Toast.LENGTH_SHORT).show();
                        }
                    }
                });
    }
}
```

Step 5: Create HomeActivity.java for the home screen after login:

```java
// HomeActivity.java
public class HomeActivity extends AppCompatActivity {

    @Override
    protected void onCreate(Bundle savedInstanceState) {
        super.onCreate(savedInstanceState);
        setContentView(R.layout.activity_home);
    }
}
```

Step 6: Add HomeActivity to the Manifest:

- Open the AndroidManifest.xml file and add the following entry:

```xml
<activity android:name=".HomeActivity" />
```

Ensure that you have the necessary XML layouts for activity_home.xml.

Now, you have a basic login/register page with Firebase Authentication. Customize the code and layout as needed for your specific requirements.

Sources and References

Online Documentation and Guides:

1. Android Developer Documentation

https://developer.android.com/docs

Official documentation provided by the Android team, covering a wide range of topics related to Android development.

2. Material Design Guidelines

https://material.io/design

Guidelines and resources for implementing Material Design principles in Android apps.

Research Papers and Journals:

1. "A Study of Android Application Security"

Authors: William Enck, Damien Octeau, Patrick McDaniel, and Swarat Chaudhuri

Published in the 20th USENIX Security Symposium (2011).

Forums and Community Discussions:

1. Stack Overflow

https://stackoverflow.com

An online community where developers seek and share solutions to programming challenges. Specific threads have been referenced for troubleshooting and best practices.

2. Reddit - r/androiddev

https://www.reddit.com/r/androiddev

Community discussions and insights from Android developers worldwide.

About the Authors

Writing this book was a passion project, and your engagement makes it all worthwhile. I hope the insights shared prove valuable in your Android journey, whether you're a beginner or an experienced developer.

Thank you for your time and trust. Here's to your continued success in the exciting realm of Android development!

Prem Kumar, an influential figure in the Indian IT industry, discovered his passion for computers during a pivotal era of industry evolution. Graduating in Computer Science Engineering, he furthered his studies and began his journey as an author with the acclaimed book "Getting Inside Java: Beginner's Guide," earning recognition from the India Book of Records in 2021.

As an IT professional, Prem has remained at the forefront of technology. Beyond his role as an author, he is a respected speaker and columnist, sharing his insights on various tech subjects. In 2019, Microsoft recognized his contributions with the prestigious "Microsoft Technology Associate" award for Java Programming.

In addition to his notable achievements, Prem Kumar is also a best-selling author, gaining acclaim for his second book, "Web Design with HTML & CSS: HTML & CSS Complete Beginner's Guide."

For a glimpse into Prem Kumar's dynamic journey and his ongoing contributions to the tech field, feel free to contact him at premkmr1611@gmail.com.

Archana Panda, a distinguished individual with a Masters in Computer Science, holds the esteemed position of Assistant Professor. Beyond her academic pursuits, she has ventured into the world of authorship, contributing her expertise to the field of computer science and technology.

With a robust academic background, Archana brings a wealth of knowledge and insights to her role as an Assistant Professor. Her contributions extend beyond the classroom, as she actively engages in sharing her expertise through the written word.

As an author, Archana has likely contributed to publications or written works related to computer science, technology, or academic research. Her commitment to both academia and the dissemination of knowledge underscores her passion for advancing the field.

For a deeper understanding of Archana Panda's contributions and insights, exploring her written works or academic publications would provide valuable insights into her expertise and areas of focus within the realm of computer science.